Schools That Succeed

Schools
That
Succeed

HOW EDUCATORS MARSHAL
THE POWER OF SYSTEMS
FOR IMPROVEMENT

KARIN CHENOWETH

HARVARD EDUCATION PRESS
CAMBRIDGE, MASSACHUSETTS

Paperback ISBN 978-1-68253-027-6
Library Edition ISBN 978-1-68253-028-3

Library of Congress Cataloging-in-Publication Data
Names: Chenoweth, Karin, author.
Title: Schools that succeed : how educators marshal the power of systems for
    improvement / Karin Chenoweth.
Description: Cambridge, Massachusetts : Harvard Education Press, ?2017. |
    Includes bibliographical references and index.
Identifiers: LCCN 2016047027| ISBN 9781682530276 (pbk.) | ISBN 9781682530283
    (library edition)
Subjects: LCSH: School improvement programs—United States—Case studies. |
    Academic achievement—United States—Case studies. | Educational
    accountability—United States—Case studies. | Educational
    leadership—United States—Case studies. | Low-income
    students—Education—United States—Case studies. |
    Minorities—Education—United States—Case studies.
Classification: LCC LB1062.6 .C483 2017 | DDC 371.2/07--dc23
LC record available at https://lccn.loc.gov/2016047027

Published by Harvard Education Press,
an imprint of the Harvard Education Publishing Group

Harvard Education Press
8 Story Street
Cambridge, MA 02138

Cover Design: Wilcox Design
Cover Image: Gregor Schuster/Photographer's Choice RF/Getty Images

The typefaces used in this book are Hoefler Text, Univers Condensed, and Gotham.

To all the educators who keep alive the dream
of an educated citizenry improving and
perfecting our democracy. A lot depends on you.

Contents

What We Can Learn from Experts

It Takes Systems

Over the last twenty years the national conversation about schools and education has gone from complacent to frantic. Where once we argued about whether schools must improve, today it seems as if just about everyone has an idea for The One Thing that will reinvent, disrupt, and transform education.

Governance changes, reading programs, advanced technology, evaluation systems, "grit," even "mindfulness" all have adherents claiming great powers of transforming schools. No end of programs and fixes are proposed and tried. But even solutions that seem to be successful in one school or district are hopeless failures in another. With no agreed-upon way forward, we seem to be left with an endless churn of debate, recrimination, and increasingly extreme policy proposals.

Yet, all over the country are educators who—quietly and without much fanfare—have figured out how to make schools better. Not just a little better. A lot better. They are ordinary educators in many respects, but they have found ways to marshal the power of schools to help students in a way that seems impossible elsewhere. They are transforming institutions into vibrant places of learning and growth—places where teachers want to teach and children want to learn—and in the process they are keeping the American Dream alive for the next generation.

For more than a decade, I have found such educators by going to regular neighborhood schools that, given their demographics, are expected to be mediocre or low performing. That is to say, they are schools that do not select or screen their students, most of whom are students of color or students who come from low-income families. These schools perform at least as well as white, middle-class schools. Sometimes they perform at the top of their states.

It never fails to amaze me: I walk into schools because of a bunch of numbers, and inside I find passionate, knowledgeable, skillful educators who believe their students are capable of great things and figure out how to teach them.

Many education researchers and commentators call such schools "outliers" and dismiss them as statistical anomalies. This strikes me as bizarre thinking. No engineer in the early twentieth century would have dismissed the Brooklyn Bridge as an outlier. Instead, bridge engineers studied it for the lessons it held. And then they built the even longer Verrazano-Narrows Bridge.

Of course, part of the problem is that measurement in education is much slipperier than in engineering. What does it mean for a school to be high performing? Not everyone thinks that the standardized tests we use to see if students can read, write, and do math on grade level are good measures. I would never argue that test scores provide a complete story about a school—no one who has spent time hanging around schools would. But as flawed as they may be, state assessment results provide some baseline idea of how well students are reading and doing math or whatever else is tested; and they, along with graduation rates, give us the only real way to compare across classrooms, schools, and districts. Now that many states are in assessment consortia, we can even compare schools in different states.

It is worth remembering that until we had publicly available data that broke out achievement by schools and demographic groups, the only way we could know anything about what was going on in a school was by physically entering it and walking into every classroom—and even that would yield only brief snapshots of what the school was like.

Now we can, relatively easily, find schools that outperform their peers and then learn from them.

MINING THE WEALTH OF KNOWLEDGE AND EXPERTISE

In deliberately seeking out such outliers—I call them "unexpected schools"—I have stumbled upon an amazing vein of educational knowledge, expertise, and skill.

My first attempt to mine this wealth was in *It's Being Done: Academic Success in Unexpected Schools* (2007), which documented the existence of unexpected schools by profiling fifteen schools and one group of schools that were either high performing or rapidly improving.

Back then, people could point to few examples of successful schools that serve students of color and students from low-income homes. Although there had been a rich line of research into what were called "effective schools" in the 1970s and 1980s, it had mostly been forgotten. Most of what the public heard was about highly successful wealthy schools and failing poor schools. The term *low-achieving urban schools* had become synonymous with schools that served black and Hispanic children from low-income families. The few counterexamples that were in the public eye were charter and magnet schools that in some way selected their students. *It's Being Done* provided stories of what were for the most part regular neighborhood schools that struggle with the same issues as other schools but had figured out some solutions.

I identified twenty-five characteristics that I observed were common to the schools, ranging from "they have high expectations for students" to "they are nice places to work." But many educators complained that I had given too little in the way of concrete details about how the schools operated.

I responded with *HOW It's Being Done: Urgent Lessons from Unexpected Schools (2009)*, in which I profiled eight high performing schools—all with large populations of students of color or students living in poverty. Like the schools profiled in *It's Being Done,* the schools differed in all kinds of characteristics that are sometimes thought to be important. They were big, small, urban, rural, suburban, racially or economically isolated and integrated, elementary and secondary. But in studying them in greater depth, I found they all shared five basic processes:

- They focused closely on what students need to learn.
- They collaborated on how to teach it.

- They assessed frequently to see if students learned it.
- They used data to find patterns and adjust instruction.
- They built relationships.

Nothing is weird or counterintuitive about any of those processes. Each is rooted as deeply in educational research, craft knowledge, and common sense as it is possible to be, and educators around the country aspire to institute all of them. But as simple as those processes are to describe, none of them are easy to do or to put in place, which raised the question of how the educators in those schools had learned to make those processes work meaningfully. At the end of *HOW It's Being Done*, I remarked rather casually that principals seemed to be important.

That statement was hardly daring. It might be theoretically possible for a school to improve without strong leadership, but it is not what could be called an observed phenomenon. In a major study looking at 180 schools over nine years, Ken Leithwood's team at the University of Washington concluded in a 2010 study of school leadership:

> To date, we have not found a single case of a school improving its student achievement record in the absence of talented leadership.[1]

But that just raises the next question, which is: What does "talented leadership" mean?

To try to answer that question, I worked with then-director of research at The Education Trust, Christina Theokas, to study thirty-three principals and assistant principals in twenty-four of the schools that had been profiled in the previous two books and a few additional schools to better understand the role of school leadership. That partnership resulted in *Getting It Done: Leading Academic Success in Unexpected Schools* (2011). Briefly, we found that principals of unexpected schools all share a strong belief in the capacity of all their students, which drives them to do the hard work to ensure the success of their students.

Make no mistake. It is hard work to take in hundreds—sometimes thousands—of children and help all of them meet commonly accepted academic standards. It is difficult even when students come in well prepared and well supported by their families, much less when they arrive behind and come from difficult family circumstances. Even some of the leaders in unexpected schools occasionally quail at the magnitude of the task they have undertaken. They do what they can because, as one said to me, "we're the only hope they've got." As they demonstrate, what they can do is quite a lot.

CONFRONTING THE TRADITIONAL WAY SCHOOLS ARE ORGANIZED

I have often found, in talking with teachers in what I call "normal" schools, that they are flummoxed by my descriptions. For example, when I say that in unexpected schools professional development is linked to both the individual needs of teachers and school goals and driven by classroom observations by principals and other school leaders, they will say something to the effect of, "The only time I see my principal is when he's doing a walk-through."

Sometimes I will describe how teachers, together, unpack standards, map out the curriculum, and develop common assessments and the lessons that lead up to them. The conversation stopper: "We don't have common planning times."

In those conversations I have realized there is yet another layer of meaning to be found in unexpected schools, which is that the educators in them have confronted the way schools are organized.

A classic essay on how schools have traditionally been organized was written by Harvard education professor Richard Elmore.[2] When I first read it, I felt the way I did when I went up in an airplane for the first time. I was seeing the same terrain but from a completely new, transformative, perspective. His basic analysis was the fact that teaching has primarily been an isolated, autonomous, idiosyncratic practice puts it completely at odds with any ability to improve schools. As Elmore said, "Privacy of practice produces isolation; isolation is the enemy of improvement." As long as school leaders allowed teaching to be a private activity, Elmore argued, school improvement would be impossible.

When the core technology of schools is buried in the individual decisions of classroom teachers and buffered from external scrutiny, outcomes are the consequence of mysterious processes that no one understands at the collective, institutional level. Therefore, school people and the public at large are free to assign causality to whatever their favorite theory suggests: weak family structures, poverty, discrimination, lack of aptitude, peer pressure, diet, television, etc.[3]

As if to prove Elmore's point, an enormous amount of research in the past fifty years has focused on what students themselves bring to the process—whether their parents are educated, what their family income is, how many books they have in their home, the influence of hip-hop, and so forth. Endless replications demonstrate that—on average—as family socioeconomic status decreases, so does academic achievement.[4]

Disrupting that pattern, Elmore argued, would require organizing schools very differently to open up the teaching process to scrutiny and thus improvement.

That type of reorganization is what I have seen in these outlier schools. By organizing schools in ways that support all the processes I identified in *HOW It's Being Done*—in other words, opening the teaching process to scrutiny and thus improvement—they have been able to disrupt the tight correlation of academic achievement and socioeconomic status.

That is what this book is about.

In the chapters that follow, I will report on my observations of educators who understand how to confront the ways in which schools have been traditionally organized and change them in ways that sometimes seem very simple and yet have profound implications for teaching and learning. I need to make something clear: this is not easy work. For one thing, it requires questioning established systems, which in turn means making people uncomfortable. Schools are human institutions, and they develop ways of operating that are familiar and have a certain logic, even if they're not efficient or successful.

I am convinced that Elmore was right: as long as schools are organized in traditional ways, schools will be entirely dependent on the social capital students bring to their schooling. Schools serving low-income families will for the most part be low performing; schools serving middle-class and upper-middle-class families will appear to be reasonably successful. But I would argue that far too often such schools' overall success masks significant organizational weakness. Because their students bring with them large vocabularies, substantial background knowledge, and parents who notice and fill in gaps in instruction, high-wealth schools often feel no sense of urgency about improvement and as a result often don't serve their students as well as they could. Such schools' organizational weakness often becomes exposed if their demographics change. Schools that go, say, from serving mostly white middle-class students to serving mostly low-income students or new immigrants are often revealed as institutions that are not in and of themselves "good schools." Rather, they were schools that hadn't needed to marshal their full power as institutions because they had relied on the strength of their students.

We don't generally talk about this issue. The general assessment often is that poor kids and kids of color cause schools to "go downhill." Their parents don't care, they aren't academically inclined, they're exceptionally disruptive—the list of things that is said goes on and on. I saw this type of thinking in the high school my children attended. The once predominantly white, middle-class school had experienced a large increase in low-income students and students of color whose families had been drawn to the area in part by the good reputation of the schools. Many of the faculty and staff openly talked of hoping the good kids would come back and watched neighborhood housing sales to see if their return was imminent. What they *didn't* do was examine their practices to see what needed to change. The dull march through boring and dated textbooks and the tedium of poorly thought-through worksheets continued unabated in many classrooms as it had for decades—and there were no structures in the school that challenged those practices.

That is to say, there was no systematic way to make sure teachers knew what the state standards required students to know; there was no systematic way to ensure that teachers taught to the standards; there was no systematic way to identify those students who had not mastered state standards; and there was no systematic way to recognize which teachers were doing a better job than others so they could help their colleagues. Some individual teachers worked hard to master the standards, curriculum, and pedagogy and develop strong relationships with students; but there was no system to ensure they did. This meant that kids who didn't have the vocabulary, background knowledge, and organizational wherewithal to compensate for the weak school structures did not, on average, fare well. Some teachers were able to help individual students but by themselves were unable to disrupt the well-worn pattern of academic achievement tightly correlating with family income and ethnicity.

Those weaknesses seem crystal clear after spending time in unexpected schools, but recognizing them requires seeing past the surface of the way schools operate. I talk with many unexpected school leaders who host visitors from other schools and, after showing them around their schools—and talking with them at great length about all the things their schools do—see the visitors take away a small, trivial piece that doesn't in any way challenge them to do things substantially differently. The visitors will, for example, leave resolved to implement the same policy regarding student dress codes as the unexpected school, or buy the specific brand of computers it uses, or adopt a particular math or reading program. On one level this behavior amuses the leaders, but on another it deeply frustrates them. They know that, as almost all of them have told me at one time or another, "It's not about a program."

In this book I am trying to convey what these school leaders do think it's about.

A JOURNEY THROUGH AMERICAN EDUCATION

Each of the schools and districts I write about could be the subject of its own book. Each has a complicated and in some ways dramatic tale to tell. By gathering all these stories together, I cannot hope to tell everything important about each of them. Rather, I am hoping to provide readers an opportunity to, in essence, accompany me on the remarkable journey through American education I have been lucky enough to take.

Chapters 1–3: Learning from High Achievement

Chapter 1, "Finding and Uncovering Expertise: Artesia High School, Lakewood, California," describes in some detail the process I used to find Artesia High School—a high-poverty school in Los Angeles County—to give an insight into how it is possible to find schools to learn from through the data. It then describes the remarkable school that I uncovered through the data.

Chapter 2, "'It's Not Just That': Systems at Malverne High School, Malverne, New York," describes Malverne High School—a working-class school in Nassau County where most of the students are African American—that is performing at a very high level.

Chapter 3, "How Malverne Became Malverne: Replicating Expertise at Elmont Memorial High School, Elmont, New York," profiles Elmont Memorial High School, which in many ways was Malverne's antecedent and demonstrates how high performance can be sustained over many years. The first time I wrote about Elmont was in *It's Being Done* back in 2007, so this is an opportunity to revisit a school that has taught me a great deal about school improvement.

Chapters 4–6: Learning from Improvement

I long ago realized that for educators in regular or low performing schools to read about what I call unexpected schools can be somewhat intimidating. By the time I usually get there, schools have so many systems, initiatives, and processes in place that it is understandable for educators in low performing schools to throw up their hands and say that there is no way they can even think about emulating them.

With that thought in mind, in 2012 I began a process of visiting and observing a small number of schools where expert leaders took on new jobs in low performing schools to lead improvement. In this book I give a few examples to try to convey what the work of school improvement is like as it happens. In the process it is possible to see just how badly organized some schools are and how the ways they are organized undermines student learning.

Chapter 4, "Starting from Scratch: Dr. Robert W. Gilliard Elementary School, Mobile, Alabama," describes the work of Debbie Bolden as she took a school that was widely described as a "hellhole" to a well-established, reasonably achieving school poised for greater success.

Chapter 5, "Experts and Their Systems at Work: Four Stories," describes the work of several other principals as they begin the improvement process.

Chapter 6, "Why Expertise Is Not Enough: A Cautionary Tale," describes the work of Ricardo Leblanc-Esparza and the difficulties he encountered both within the schools he led and in the larger context of his districts. The first time I wrote about Esparza was in *It's Being Done*, where I profiled the high-poverty high school he led, Granger High School. This chapter demonstrates the way districts can undermine improvement.

Chapter 7: Could There Be "Unexpected Districts" as Well as Unexpected Schools?

Chapter 6 raised a big question: What kind of ecosystem supports schools in their improvement efforts? That is to say, what systems can school districts and states put in place to support school improvement? This is a hugely important question. I only begin to explore it in this chapter that features Delaware's Indian River School District.

Chapter 8: Marshaling the Power of Schools

In Chapter 8 I draw on all the previous chapters—and the previous books— to identify the key systems that distinguish all the high performing and rapidly improving schools and districts I have observed.

The educators in unexpected schools, like engineers, have worked the problems that face them by drawing on research and craft knowledge— and by stealing good ideas wherever they find them. In the process they make sure that the ways they schedule time, organize information, handle student behavior, spend money, develop the leadership capacity of their teachers and staff, even how they arrange the physical space of their buildings are all focused on improving teaching and learning. They do this because they know, deep in their bones, their students are able to achieve and they are determined to help them.

CHAPTER ONE

Finding and Uncovering Expertise

Artesia High School, Lakewood, Los Angeles

As I said in the introduction, it never fails to amaze me the way a bunch of numbers on a page burst into reality as wonderful schools with passionate, dedicated, and expert educators.

The most recent example of that for me is Artesia High School in Los Angeles County, California.

Before I describe Artesia, however, I would like to share the process of how I identified it to give an insight into how this process of learning from unexpected schools can work.

I should first say that the last couple of years have been a little tough on the school-identification-by-data business because most states have been changing their assessments and reporting systems.

NAVIGATING THE NEW ASSESSMENTS

To give a little context, what follows is a thumbnail history of why we even have assessments and how they have been changing.

In 1965, the passage of the Elementary and Secondary Education Act (ESEA) as part of the War on Poverty meant that large amounts of federal money started being funneled to schools with students living in poverty, mainly through Title I of the act. The idea was that Title I money would provide the resources—additional teachers, teachers' aides, extra time, and materials—that would equalize the education of children living in poverty and children from middle-class homes. There were a lot of strictures to make sure the money was being spent on poor children, but there was no mechanism built in to see if that money was making a difference.

Here's a little-known piece of trivia from that time: During the hearings for the bill, Senator Robert F. Kennedy (D-Massachusetts) argued that there should be some accountability for that money. One of the things he said was:

> I think it is very difficult for a person who lives in a community to know whether, in fact, his educational system is what it should be, whether if you compare his community to a neighboring community they are doing everything they should do, whether the people that are operating the educational system in a state or in a local community are as good as they should be. I think it is very difficult for a citizen to know that. So you come in and say, "We have a certain percentage of economically deprived children in a particular district. We are going to put up $2 million there."
>
> Now, that $2 million, because of the kind of [school] board you have there, might be completely wasted while $2 million in some other community might be used to help a child tremendously. If I lived in a community where the $2 million was being wasted, I would like to know something about that. I would like—I wonder if we couldn't just have some kind of system of reporting, either through some testing system which could be established which the people at the local community would know periodically as to what progress had been made under this program. I think it would be very helpful to Congress and I think it would be very helpful to people living in the states, and I think it would be very helpful to people living in the local community.[1]

Kennedy's desire for accountability for Title I money was pretty much ignored, and the money poured out from the federal government, through states, to schools.

The next two decades saw considerable progress in children's reading and math achievement.[2] The long-term National Assessment of Educational Progress (NAEP), which sampled students all over the country, showed improvement across the board but particularly for poor children and African American and Hispanic children, which meant that for years there was significant narrowing of gaps in achievement among groups. That progress essentially stopped right around 1988 when the achievement of poor children and children of color began to stagnate in math and actually lost ground in reading. Was Title I money the reason for the improved achievement? If so, why did progress stop in 1988? I don't know that anyone has a definitive answer to either question, though a lot of hypotheses float around.

In any case, alarmed by the undoing of the progress that had been made and presented with evidence that Title I monies weren't always being used in effective ways, the U.S. Congress passed and President Bill W. Clinton signed the 1994 iteration of ESEA, which required states that choose to receive Title I money (all of them do) to establish standards for what all students should learn and measure whether they were learning it. This requirement was an attempt to see if Title I monies were being used appropriately, somewhat along the lines of what Kennedy had suggested. All states were supposed to test students three times during their school careers in reading and math and report results to parents and the community by school and demographic group; but the Clinton administration granted so many waivers that although many states were testing, by 2001 only eleven states were reporting results by demographic group.

That's when the No Child Left Behind (NCLB) iteration of ESEA was passed, this time requiring

- testing against state standards in reading and math from third through eighth grade and once in high school, with an additional science test thrown in; and
- reporting the results overall and by demographic group for each school.

Because of this requirement, by 2005 or so, it was possible for anyone to look up the results on just about every school in the country online. Some states reported results in clear, understandable ways; some states didn't. But it was possible to see school results, and it was also possible to compare schools within states.

Because every state had its own standards and its own tests, it wasn't possible to compare schools across states. It was, however, possible to compare how states as a whole compared against each other. The reason was that all states were now required to participate in NAEP testing under NCLB.

Those state-by-state NAEP comparisons proved to be pretty embarrassing to some states, especially because they made it crystal clear that some states expected students to learn much less than others did. If, for example, a state reported that 90 percent of its students were proficient readers, and NAEP reported that only 30 percent were, that result indicated the state wasn't expecting much in the way of proficient reading.

States' embarrassment helped jumpstart a process whereby they began developing reading and math standards that would be common. One of the many reasons they undertook this work was that the tests most states used were low-level, cheap, multiple-choice tests that were nothing like the National Assessment of Educational Progress. If states had common standards, the reasoning went, they would have the resources to join together to create more sophisticated, expensive tests whose results would better match those of NAEP. And that's what they did, with forty-seven states adopting what came to be called Common Core State Standards. Many states joined two assessment consortia, PARCC and Smarter Balanced, which took several years to develop new tests. The two assessments have different ways of measuring, but both are definitely more sophisticated than the old tests. Their results are certainly closer to NAEP results than the previous tests.

States began piloting the new assessments in 2013 and 2014, accompanied by a lot of technical glitches because they were mostly administered by computer instead of paper and pencil. In addition, huge political fights emerged over both the Common Core State Standards and the assessments. At this writing, forty-three states plus the District of Columbia and four territories are still part of Common Core, but only eleven states are part of PARCC and fifteen part of Smarter Balanced. Arkansas is an example of a state that started as a PARCC state but, partly because of testing glitches and partly because of unhappiness over the test itself, switched to ACT Aspire—which is yet another national assessment. ACT Aspire is designed to assess whether students are on track to succeed on the ACT college application exam when students take it in tenth grade.

Whether students take PARCC, Smarter Balanced, ACT Aspire, or New York's separate Common Core tests, results don't look the same as under the old state tests. A school where 90 percent of students met or exceeded state standards on the old state tests all of a sudden has only 40 or 50 percent considered proficient. The reason isn't that the students are learning less; it's that the measure changed.

The new tests, in other words, are quite a bit harder and have proven to be a shock.

To bring us up to date, in 2015 the new iteration of ESEA—the Every Student Succeeds Act—kept the testing and reporting rules established by No Child Left Behind. Even though there are issues with assessments and some of the ways states report the results—and I have issues with both— they still provide critical information and a way to find schools to learn from. Even when proficiency rates don't look impressive, it is still possible to compare how individual schools do in comparison to average results for schools in their states. A school with a 40 percent proficiency rate on the fifth grade state math test, for example, looks terrible—until you realize that the state proficiency rate is 25 percent.

Probably the most efficient way to find schools that are performing at unexpectedly high levels is to download state results into an Excel sheet and then start systematically sorting—by demographic group, by achievement, by graduation rates, and so forth. I've never mastered that process. I prefer to do what I call spelunking through the data.

This brings us to Artesia.

FINDING ARTESIA

I am always on the alert for news stories about promising schools and districts, and many years ago the American Federation of Teachers—the smaller of the two national teacher unions—announced that its local had developed a partnership with the ABC Unified School District, in part to resolve bitterness following a strike and in part to try to close the district's significant achievement gaps.[3] The AFT's descriptions of collaboration sounded promising, but when I looked at the district's data the first few years after the announcement, my basic reaction was, "meh." Whenever I hear about initiatives, programs, disruptions, reinventions, and so forth,

I always start with the data and I'm often unimpressed. So I wasn't surprised but also wasn't particularly interested.

Time elapsed and I decided to check back in.[4] This time the initial data looked promising. The district, a combination of three smaller districts in Los Angeles County east and south of the city, has about twenty-one thousand students, half of them meeting the qualifications for free and reduced-price meals. On the new Smarter Balanced assessment that California administers, the district was outperforming the state as a whole and its African American, Hispanic, and low-income students were outperforming their counterparts in the state in both English language arts and math.

In searching for more information, I found an article that said many of the district's improvement efforts had been aimed at its "Southside" schools, where most of the children are either Hispanic or African American from low-income families. The union and the district had joined together to provide a great deal of training in reading instruction and leadership for the Southside schools, and I looked at the data for those schools. They were doing much better than I remembered them doing years before, but my attention was drawn to Artesia High School, which was performing just a bit below the rest of the district.

One thing I should note is that high schools are tough to improve, for a lot of reasons. The way most of them are set up is to take kids where they are and keep them right there. If students come in high performing, they are sent into advanced classes; if they come in low performing, they are sent into low-level classes. And that's usually that. Often there's no way for students to move up. In addition, the departmental structure of high schools often inures them to the kinds of collaboration and improvement that elementary school teachers seem more inclined to embrace.

Because I was intrigued by Artesia High School, I started looking at its data in more detail. It has more than one thousand five hundred students, 72 percent of whom are Hispanic, 9 percent African American, 7 percent Filipino, and 4 percent white. Almost 80 percent are considered by the state to be "socioeconomically disadvantaged," making it the highest poverty high school in the district.

Then I looked at the school's graduation rates, and they were eye-popping. The most recent data when I looked was for 2014, and 98 percent of all students graduated that year; 100 percent of the school's African

American students; and 96 percent of English language learners. To give a comparison, in the rest of Los Angeles County, students graduated at a rate of 78 percent, and in California they graduate at a rate of 81 percent. Statewide, African Americans graduated at a rate of 68 percent in 2014; English language learners at a rate of 63 percent.

It seemed clear that something was going on at Artesia. I wondered what previous years' data would show.

Graduation rates are hard to compare in previous years, because before federal requirements under No Child Left Behind kicked in, every state had its own definition for what constituted its graduation rate. Since 2007 California has reported what is called a "cohort graduation rate," which counts the percentage of students who enter as freshmen who graduate four years later. In the past California simply used to report the number of seniors who graduated, ignoring what may have happened to all the students who left before their senior year. Still, the number the state reported is instructive—only about 80 percent of Artesia's seniors graduated in 2003, 2004, and 2005. Considering that students who are unlikely to graduate usually drop out before the senior year, 80 percent was less than impressive.

I dug a little further into the previous assessment system. Until 2013, California gave its state-specific STAR and CAHSEE tests, the results of which it rolled up into what it called the Academic Performance Index, or API. The API was on a 1,000-point scale, with 600 being quite low-performing and 1,000 being mathematically impossible to achieve.[5] The state established 800 as the standard all schools should aspire to, and usually only wealthy schools exceeded that. Just to give an example that non-Californians might recognize, Beverly Hills High School, which is quite a wealthy school, had an API of 865 in 2013.

Artesia's API in 2013 was 777—not quite at the standard, but still good enough to earn it the designation of California Distinguished School. Whites, Asians, and Filipinos were above 800, and African American, Hispanic, and socioeconomically disadvantaged students were below, but they were all above 750. Even English language learners were at 723. The biggest gap in achievement was with students with disabilities, whose API was 577. Artesia seemed to have a fairly high percentage of students with disabilities—16 percent.

FIGURE 1–1

Artesia High School Graduation Rates, 2015

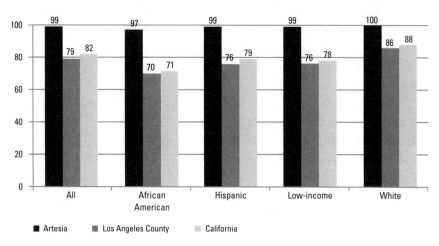

Source: California Department of Education
Data shown are four-year cohort grauation rates

Then I looked at how those groups compared with the same groups across the state, and all the largest demographic groups at Artesia were out-performing their counterparts in the state. So, for example, students with disabilities statewide in 2013 had an API of 532 in California as a whole; English language learners, 651; African Americans, 666; Hispanics, 709.

I wondered if Artesia had always performed at this level, so I looked at the previous ten years of data and saw a remarkable trajectory of improvement. In 2003, its API was 576. To have grown 200 points, from 576 to 777, was unusual. To draw it out just a bit more, in 2003 the school as a whole had been performing at the same level as students with disabilities in 2013.

"YOU HAVE NO IDEA THE SMILE ON MY FACE"

I definitely wanted to know more, so I called the school.

When I told the secretary I wanted to talk with someone about the school's improvement over the past few years, she connected me to the dean, Rosi Gomez, who was delighted to tell me that she herself had attended the school as a student, and today's Artesia was "very different" from the way it was back then. I tried to get more of a sense of what had changed, but she said I really needed to talk with the principal, Sergio Garcia, who called me back later that day.

I asked Garcia a few initial questions—how long he had been there, whether the demographics of the school had changed over the years, and so forth. It turned out that he had been there since 2005 and, he said, the main changes in demographics were that the school now had more students with disabilities, English language learners, and students who qualify for free and reduced-price meals than when he started. The district website said Artesia was a magnet school, but Garcia said that that was an old designation from a grant that had run out before he arrived.

Then I got to the main question: From the data it looked as if the school had been a bit of a mess back in 2005. What was the school doing differently now than ten years ago?

"You have no idea the smile on my face," he said. "No one has ever asked me that question before."

I booked a flight as soon as I was able and headed to Los Angeles County.

The school itself is unprepossessing—like many California schools, it consists of one-story buildings that house groups of classrooms, so students go outdoors when they travel from class to class and eat in the public square created by the buildings. It is located in a somewhat featureless neighborhood surrounded by housing and strip malls.

Inside its confines I found teachers and students who were enthusiastic about being there. Everywhere I looked, I saw students learning. I saw them debating evidence of climate change; analyzing *To Kill a Mockingbird;* identifying whether liquids were acid or base; comparing the Industrial Revolution to the French Revolution; and calculating the force needed to push a piano up a ramp. I saw classes aimed at helping students get jobs in the biomedical industry; and I heard about plans to make the career and technical classes more cohesive and comprehensive so that students would be well set up to obtain a technical certification after high school in a variety of fields.

I saw, in other words, a high school that was focused on providing students with a comprehensive education and preparing them for life after high school. I didn't talk to a single student who wasn't planning on attending some kind of college, and every senior I spoke to had applied and was waiting to hear from the admissions offices of four-year colleges or had already settled on what two-year college to enroll in. All the students I talked to said they were learning a great deal, and almost all of them volunteered that they felt "safe."

This description may seem unremarkable to anyone who has only spent time in a high school that mostly serves middle-class and upper-middle-class students. But high-poverty schools are often places to see adults and students pitted against each other; watch time being wasted in endless permutations; and find students who have only the vaguest idea of what they will be doing after high school and are uneasy about being in school.

How was it possible for a school where 80 percent of students live in low-income families to perform comparably to middle-class schools? That was the question I wanted to answer.

As with all unexpected schools, the details of Artesia's story are complex and nuanced—what university academicians might call "highly contextualized." But Artesia has underlying patterns that I recognized from many other unexpected schools.

THE DISTRICT CONTEXT

Although there are other partnerships between unions and school districts, the ABC Unified compact with its union, ABCFT, is one of the oldest and most successful. Begun after a bitter strike in the 1990s, it has lasted through three superintendents, two union presidents, and several school board elections. Its longevity has allowed it to be institutionalized into the operation of the district. Every department head in central administration has a union counterpart, and they meet regularly; the union and district people hold annual retreats; and union and district people undergo some of the same training in leadership and how to improve instruction, with a great deal of focus on improving reading instruction. Both the local and the national union, the American Federation of Teachers, have put in their own money for training and conference attendance, and union and district people regularly speak about the collaboration at conferences around the country.

Gary Smuts, who was the second superintendent to be part of the compact, said that when the president of the AFT, Randi Weingarten, visited Artesia High School, she said after the meeting, "It just dawned on me—other than Sergio, I can't tell who's a teacher and who's management—and that's delightful."

Smuts credits the partnership with developing a "critical mass that produces a lot of creative energy." Ray Gaer, the district union president, said that originally he thought the partnership was "just a way to improve relationships. Now I think it's a way to turn around a district."

Another piece of the district context is that while Artesia was improving, so was the feeder pattern—that is, the elementary and middle schools that feed into Artesia. So, for example, Fedde Middle School, whose students feed into Artesia, went from having an API of 593 in 2003 to having an API of 729 in 2013. In other words, Artesia's improvement does not appear to be isolated but is part of a district process.

All that is important context, but I'm going to focus on what happened at Artesia.

"SYSTEMS WITHIN SYSTEMS"

Garcia began work in the summer of 2005 after Artesia had had a principal who, in the words of union president Gaer, "broke the staff." Gaer had started teaching at Artesia as a young man under the previous principal who "walked on water," Gaer said. But the next principal had walked in and "within five minutes told us everything we did was wrong." After five years, achievement was low, discipline was out of control, and teacher morale was terrible.

Smuts, who at the time was deputy superintendent, had the job of finding a replacement when the previous principal took a job elsewhere. He had heard about Garcia because there was a lot of public turmoil, including teacher walkouts, in the school he was leading at the time. Smuts went to see for himself. "Half the staff liked him and half the staff didn't," Smuts said. He interviewed teachers in both camps and was struck by the fact that Garcia's biggest critic told him, "You know, Sergio is right. We don't like him, but he's right." Smuts decided that Garcia's main problem was that he hadn't been properly supported by his district, so Smuts offered him the job at Artesia.

Garcia lived just a few minutes away from Artesia, and he thought the shorter commute would make life easier by giving him more time to spend with his two young daughters. Then he toured the school and saw five fights in twenty minutes. His first thought: "What have I gotten myself into?" His second: "I can really help this school."

Within Artesia's catchment area was one of the most notorious gang territories in the country—Hawaiian Gardens. The dominant gang, VHG, would in 2009 be the target of the largest law enforcement raid in history. This was after the gang had conducted a systematic campaign to rid the community of African Americans through murder and intimidation and one of the gang's leaders killed a Los Angeles sheriff. That year the FBI estimated that one in every fifteen people who lived in Hawaiian Gardens was connected to VHG.[6]

Some of the community turmoil inevitably spilled over to Artesia. "We had gangs in the yard intimidating people," Gerry Ellis, who chairs the physical education department, told me. Another long-time teacher said that he hadn't wanted his wife to visit him at school for fear of the language and behavior she would be subjected to.

In the summer of 2005, Garcia had even more pressing concerns. A veteran of high schools, Garcia knew that the school had what he called "systems within systems within systems," and he needed to master them. His general approach, he said, is that "the answers are usually within the school." But he needed to make sure the right systems were in place that would allow those answers to emerge.

"The first thing I do is look at the office to see what the office staff is like," he told me. He wanted to make sure the school secretaries made parents feel welcome. "Our parents work two or three jobs," he said. "If they come, they've made a real effort" and should be greeted with what he called "good customer service."

The next thing he does, he said, is look at the master schedule. When he saw the planned schedule for the fall, he saw what Smuts described as a "terrible mess." The previous principal had built the schedule around what Smuts called "teacher needs." So, for example, many teachers had open periods when they didn't teach; that in turn meant some classes were overcrowded.

One of the things Garcia noticed immediately about the master schedule was that very few students in the school were taking Algebra I, and many of them were sophomores and juniors. Far too many students were in consumer math or general mathematics, which was essentially middle school math. And they were failing even those classes.

Over the summer Garcia took the math department to a Sacramento high school to see how it scheduled all students in Algebra I or higher. Garcia's argument was that students needed the chance to complete a college-preparatory course of study and that meant they couldn't take their entire high school career to complete Algebra I. "I can't be at a school that perpetuates the idea that these kids will be poor the rest of their lives," he said.

The teachers were convinced and eager to get started, so he scheduled all students who would otherwise have been in lower math classes into Algebra I. This meant all the freshmen and many other students also. For those students who were clearly behind, Garcia scheduled a second class for them. In edu-speak, he double-blocked them so that they would have additional instruction to help them master the standards. Then he bought a lot of Algebra I books because the school didn't have nearly enough.

I'm kind of getting ahead of myself, but that first year, 34 percent of the 910 students who took the state Algebra I test scored basic or above on the test. That number was hardly stellar, but the school kept plugging away until, in 2013—the last year of that testing regime—pretty much the only students who were in Algebra I were freshman, and 64 percent of them scored basic or above. That number might not sound fabulous either, but it beat the state's results by four points and wasn't hugely different from Beverly Hills High School's 75 percent. Part of the increased success was due to the fact that the math department built in after-school classes to provide extra help to students.

Back to 2005—Garcia did something else with the master schedule: he ended school for students at 2 p.m. on Wednesdays to create time for teachers to be able to meet about the curriculum, and he reduced the time spent in staff meetings in favor of staff development and planning time.

Once school started, Garcia could see that "students were fighting, teachers were fighting." When he went into classrooms, however, he observed "some really good teaching." But teachers were teaching on their own with little consistency across classrooms. The question for him, he said, quickly became: "How do you get all the teachers to work together?"

At his first faculty meeting, he asked the teachers what they most wanted from him, and the answer was almost unanimous: "Stop the tardies." Teachers told him that students would wander into class late, be sent back to the office for a pass, and then arrive back again in class, so each late student represented two interruptions of instruction. Garcia took a morning to observe and saw 230 students who were late in the first twenty minutes, which gave him a sense of the magnitude of the problem.

Garcia agreed to handle the tardy problem. "But in exchange—because nothing comes for free—the teachers had to promise me they would teach bell-to-bell and show no videos unless related to the curriculum." This approach demonstrated his essential strategy, which is that instruction needed to improve even as the culture and climate needed to improve.

He set up an on-campus suspension room (OCS), which later evolved into an intervention counseling room (ICR), staffed with someone who would mentor and develop relationships with students. He then set up "sweeps" so that administrators sent all late students to the counseling room. "Within three days, we were able to get it under control," Garcia said. Now, on an average day, only about fifteen students arrive late. "A culture gets changed by changing one behavior at a time," he said.

He knew that for students to feel connected to school was something that would not happen overnight. "You've got to create relationships. But it takes time to create relationships." To gain that time, Garcia took what he called a "heavy-handed" approach to discipline, meaning that he regularly suspended students. That first year, he suspended 447 students, compared to 267 students the year before. And he still suspends students, though much less often; in the 2014–2015 school year, 122 students were suspended. But, he says, even suspended students will come to school for counseling and for sessions with an outside organization that trains students in what is called "restorative justice," which aims to have students understand how their behavior affects others and make restitution to those they have harmed.

Some teachers wanted him to, in the phrase used, "weed the garden" and expel students altogether, particularly students who were in the Hawaiian Gardens gang. "His intention never was to get rid of the bad guys," Smuts told me. "If they brought weapons and sold hard drugs, well, you have to get rid of those kids, and Sergio was nails on that." But, Smuts added, Garcia's aim was to get gang members an education. "Virtually no member of the Hawaiian Gardens gang graduated before Sergio. After he got there, after a few years, even as experienced a guy as I am couldn't tell who the Hawaiian Garden kids were. Instead of being cool to get kicked out of school, it became cool to graduate."

Garcia deeply believes that high schools need to be centers of the community, and for that reason he worked to greatly expand the school's after-school opportunities, including drama, band, clubs, and other activities that would connect the students to the school and provide what Garcia calls an "oasis" in an otherwise rather dangerous and threatening environment.

"GRITTY AND SWEATY DETAILS"

Garcia developed careful systems "for anything and everything." So, for example, a system is in place for teachers to refer students for interventions before they send students to the principal's office: three counselors provide support and see what might be going on to trigger misbehavior and acting out. "All students have at least one or two adults they can go to," is something I heard from several faculty members.

When I visited, I saw two students come into Garcia's office because they had been pushing and shoving each other. Anything resembling fighting is still taken very seriously at Artesia, but it appeared they had just been fooling around. Garcia told them their consequence for pushing and shoving was to be on clean-up duty for a few days at lunch. He told them that if they got into trouble again, he would have to take much more serious action. "Don't make me look soft," he said sternly. "We won't," the boys said.

This use of what could be called both hard and soft power is key to Garcia's approach. "When you only do the social-emotional part of discipline, these kids think you're another softie and laugh at you. But if you can take both approaches, then they respect you and learn."

Garcia takes this piece of his job extremely seriously. "The social-emotional part for me is to support them in their academics," Garcia said. "For my kids it is life and death."

But none of this was smooth sailing, and when I talked with Smuts, he was adamant that the story of Artesia include what he called "gritty and sweaty" details.

One such detail was that early on the school faced an issue of non-students jumping the fence and blending in with students. They posed real dangers to the school, in particular after there was a gang-related murder nearby. Garcia had a simple solution that he brought from another school: he had grease smeared along the top of the fence so that anyone jumping over would get dirty and, when they wiped their hands on their clothes, could be identified and escorted out. When it was mistakenly reported that he was trying to keep students in, members of the community were outraged and hundreds protested at the school board, some demanding that Garcia be fired. "I have to give them credit," Smuts said about the board. "They stood firm."

Another "gritty and sweaty" detail was that when Garcia arrived, Smuts was in the middle of investigating what he called "one of the greatest basketball scandals in the state of California." Artesia's basketball coach—who had been brought in after a previous recruiting scandal—had been part of a scheme that encompassed a great deal of Southern California, wealthy lawyers, and athletic shoe companies. "Kids would arrive on the campus in their sophomore year who were 6'6" and who had never lived anywhere near Artesia," Smuts said. Artesia was "the top-ranked basketball school in the state, but they were doing badly by the kids."

Even after the basketball coach was replaced, there were still issues about recruitment. "Sergio had the guts to see that and hire someone who only worked with local kids," Smuts said. Now the team doesn't do nearly as well in competitions, but the students go to games and support the team because they know the players, Smuts said. "Sergio pivoted to concentrate on the main purpose of school—which is educating kids," Smuts said. However, he said, some faculty and staff deeply resented that the school was no longer getting good publicity for its championship basketball team.

"MAXIMUM NUMBER OF INTERACTIONS PER MINUTE WITH COMPLEX KNOWLEDGE"

Garcia worked on academics from two separate vantage points: focusing on what teachers were doing and focusing on the motivation of students.

To work on both, Garcia brought in as a consultant someone he had worked with in previous schools, Dennis Parker. One evening Parker joined me and Garcia for dinner so that he could help explain the academic progress at Artesia. Before becoming a consultant, Parker worked for many years at the California Department of Education—including a stint as head of language arts—and for six years as a faculty member at UCLA. Since 2000 he has worked as a consultant around the state, bringing to schools a framework for what he called Strategic Schools.

Parker wants teachers to aim for students to achieve what he calls "aha!" moments. "The brain will give you an aha! moment if you process complex knowledge intensely," Parker said. To do that, he said, students need to have what he calls the "maximum number of interactions per minute with complex knowledge."

Entire departments held day-long meetings to wrestle through questions of what students needed to learn, think about how to help them struggle with difficult material, and provide a lot of accurate feedback so that students would have a clear sense of their momentum toward a goal. "As a teacher in my department, we went through the standards, discussed what primary documents we would use, what assessments we would give," said Felicia Godinez, chair of the social studies department. "It's about student achievement. We're all going to have data walls and a consolidation of practices."

By that statement, she is referring to the fact that Parker has worked with teachers to ensure they have consistent systems of instruction. So, for example, they are expected to have a way for all students to be able to respond to all questions teachers ask. That can be through hand signals, laptops, talks with each other, choral responses—Artesia's teachers use a wide variety of methods. But the idea is that students should be interacting continually in class, not simply waiting for a teacher to ask them one or two questions individually.

There is, in other words, no "program." Parker's basic improvement strategy is that at the classroom and school levels, clear performance targets need to be set, clear feedback mechanisms need to be in place, and teacher know-how needs to be developed. When those things are all working together in ways that take into account the individual classroom and school context, they spiral together to keep improvement going, Parker says. "Teachers should be helped to make better and better choices," he said. They are "less likely to oppose this kind of change, as it is helping them learn to be more effective with their students, not mandating them to follow a new regimen."

While I was at Artesia, I heard several teachers refer to Parker as "our consultant," which I took as a sign that he was accepted by the teachers there. When he and I walked through the school together, I saw teachers seek him out to tell him about some development or have students tell him about a recent triumph. Even students knew him and seemed proud to talk with him about their work. This is unusual; consultants are often drive-by workshop-givers and don't usually have that kind of acceptance among teachers, much less students. But Parker has been coming to the school for almost ten years, and he seems to be fully accepted as part of the school. In the interests of full disclosure, I should say I heard from one teacher, now retired, who deeply resented what he called Parker's insistence on specific kinds of feedback to and from students as inappropriate to his Advanced Placement students; but most teachers I spoke with seemed to think Parker had helped them improve instruction.

One of the things Parker said he helped teachers understand was that they were responsible for helping students master standards, not textbooks. Textbooks rarely match state standards, but teachers were used to marching through the textbooks. When he walks into a classroom, he immediately looks to see if the teacher has posted the standards the class is working on that quarter and what lessons have worked on those standards.

When Garcia and Parker first started at Artesia, California was still operating under its old standards and old testing regime, before Common

Core and Smarter Balanced. In their view, the old regime provided much clearer targets for teachers and students to aim for. Many people considered California's old standards to be the most comprehensive and specific set of standards in the country, and Common Core is much more focused on general skills.

"IF I GET GOOD GRADES, I'LL GET BEAT UP"

Parker observed classes and helped teachers set ambitious academic targets for their students and develop feedback mechanisms. Every classroom at Artesia has a data wall where students chart their progress on quizzes, tests, and assignments, and a space on that wall for students to add their names to those of others who are either scoring high or who have improved their performance.

If the school were only to celebrate high achievement, only a few students would be celebrated. This was especially true at the beginning of the school's improvement process—hence the insistence by Parker that both achievement and improvement be celebrated. Garcia told me that the first time he gave out T-shirts for having a high grade point average, students would stuff the shirts in their backpacks. "A kid told me that he had to get out of here. 'If I get good grades, I'll get beat up.'"

At that point, the school adopted the strategy of "mass recognition," providing students safety in numbers. Now any recognition—whether it's for attendance or grades—is designed to include as many students as is possible. So, for example, data walls in classrooms include recognition for both high achievement and improvement. "Even if the improvement is from a low F to an F+, that's improvement," Garcia said. "If students keep improving, eventually they will be achieving."

To systematize the recognition of students, the school adopted Jostens Renaissance, which is a commercial school environment program used by schools around the country. It has data and monitoring systems that help administrators keep tabs on a number of areas, including behavior, and provides lots of ways to recognize students, from providing T-shirts to handing out balloons for good or improving attendance.

"The big turnover for us is that kids want the shirts and wear them," Garcia said. The aim for the 2015–2016 school year was to have 100 percent of students apply to college and then, as they solidified their plans, they all received a T-shirt saying, "I'm going to college." By the end of the year, 37 percent of students were planning to attend four-year colleges; 60 percent, two-year colleges; and 1 percent, technical schools. The senior class earned $4.5 million in scholarships and financial aid and more than 650 students, parents, and community members attended the "I'm Going to College Dinner" that the school has held for the past four years.

Another thing Garcia did the first year was to change the way students with disabilities were treated. "That was something Sergio was brave about," union president Gaer told me. Back then Gaer was a special education teacher at Artesia. "He gave the special education department technology first—before other departments." He also scheduled students with disabilities in the regular classes with special educators providing support. "Veteran teachers weren't happy about resource teachers in their classroom, and would give [their students] fails no matter how they did."

Still, for the first time, students with disabilities had access to the core curriculum, Gaer said. "We set the expectations high and they rose to it."

Stephani Palutzke, a special educator who came a few years into Garcia's principalship, agreed. "I had worked at more of a high-achieving school where the special education students were an insignificant number. We didn't affect the scores, and we were isolated and hardly part of the school. When I came here, special ed was part of everything." Palutzke was surprised to find out that she would be expected to teach Algebra I to her students. "I can't teach a pre-algebra class? Algebra is too hard," she remembered saying to Garcia. "He said no. We found a way to teach algebra, and they passed the high school test."

And that began to answer the question why Artesia's population of students with disabilities had grown during Garcia's tenure—parents began seeking out the school for their children because they were more likely to be successful. Cecilia Perez is one such parent. "I moved [my daughter] because they have support for students with disabilities," she told me. Her daughter became the first student with learning disabilities to graduate from Artesia and enroll directly in a California State University campus. "As a parent, I was grateful," she said.

THIRTEEN PEOPLE TO DEFEND THE MASTER SCHEDULE

Right from the beginning, Garcia was working to build the school's leadership team—administrators and department chairs—so that every member would understand the procedures and systems, could help monitor them, and would suggest changes to make them more successful. "I cleared the deck some for him so he could have his own team," Smuts said, meaning that Garcia brought in his own assistant principals and dean. At this point several of Garcia's assistant principals have gone on to be principals of their own schools. Garcia thinks of being on the leadership team as being a key training time: "It's like they are in graduate school—I'm always having them read research and do book studies."

At the end of Garcia's first year, he brought the team together to create the following year's master schedule. He had built the first one, but he wanted to ensure that all the departments and administrators had a say in the next one. Besides, he said, "That way I have thirteen people to defend it."

"It took us a week that first time," said Will Napier, the chair of the special education department and one of two current union representatives of the school. "Everyone had their own program that they wanted to push. Now, we're able to do it in a couple of days, because if it doesn't work for the greater good, we know not to argue for it."

One of the most controversial scheduling decisions is to put many students who would not necessarily be considered prepared for advanced work in Advanced Placement classes. "We're putting kids in there who are not 'AP kids,'" said Cecilia Hawn, chair of the mathematics department. "We believe our kids can do whatever other kids can do," added Godinez of the social studies department. That doesn't mean they don't recognize the needs of their students. "We have a two-week AP camp in the summer to get them ready for the higher expectations; kids know they're at a huge disadvantage if they don't attend," Hawn said. They also recognized that many students don't have computers at home, which represented another disadvantage. The school established a student union with forty computers, printers, graphing calculators, and tutors that is open five days a week from 7 a.m. to 9:30 p.m.

At this point, more than half the juniors and seniors are enrolled in at least one of seventeen Advanced Placement classes, and enrollment has tripled in the last three years. Many students cannot afford to pay for the test, so the school had only 131 passing scores in 2015. But the school would rather have a student in the class and be exposed to the higher, college-level expectations than not be in the class. "We have worked really hard at providing equal access, and one of the major things I can tell you about AP is that it is open to all students and that we provide a lot of support," Garcia said.

At the same time that he was focused on Advanced Placement, Garcia became frustrated with a district policy that sent failing students to the district's "continuation" high school. Many students simply wouldn't attend because it was in rival gang territory, but those who did weren't given quality instruction, in Garcia's view. "They got credit for sitting there," he said. In 2013 he asked the superintendent, Dr. Mary Sieu, for an extra teacher and funds to set up a continuation school at Artesia. "Dr. Sieu has always supported my ideas, no matter how out-of-the-box they are," he said.

Now Garcia runs his own continuation school. "I can keep those kids here. Some of them don't know how to function in school; some have been failing since second grade and need to learn how to read or multiply. We work on the issues."

Once students are able to work at a high school level, he said, they do college-preparatory work as approved by the University of California and California State University, the two four-year university systems in the state. "You can improve a school by working at the top end or the bottom end. I refuse to do that. I work at both ends," Garcia said.

After three years, Garcia said he started to see that he was winning individual battles. It wasn't until he was five years in that he started saying, "I'm winning." At ten years, he said, "I have transformational growth. Now the teachers won't take anything less. They have their own internal accountability clock."

As I was finishing up the manuscript for this book, the results from the 2016 administration of Smarter Balanced came in, and Artesia had a nice boost, as Garcia had hoped. The school outperformed Los Angeles County and the state overall, but way outperformed the county and state for students who are African American, Hispanic, or come from low-income homes. So, for example, 69 percent of Artesia's students met or exceeded the state's English language arts standards compared to

59 percent in the state. If you only look at students from low-income families, however, 68 percent of Artesia's students met or exceeded standards compared to 48 percent in the state.

I asked Garcia to reflect on what lesson Artesia holds for other educators. "Improving Artesia wasn't rocket science. It wasn't that difficult," he said. It was a matter of understanding the "deep need" teachers have to do their job well, he said, and building the systems to help them do it.

But, he added, "It's important to mention the moral imperative that we operate under, to always do what's best for kids and to have high expectations for all students." He added that the culture of resiliency that urban communities are famous for has now moved to the academic realm where it did not exist before. "And that's what keeps me here year after year."

SYSTEMS TO NOTE

- A master schedule that
  - ensures that all students are in college-preparatory classes and that allows many students to be in Advanced Placement classes with additional support if they need it.
  - ensures that teachers have dedicated time during the school day for professional development and collaboration.
- A discipline system that uses consequences to educate students, not punish them into dropping out.
- A leadership development system that prepares people within the school to both take responsibility for systems (such as the master schedule) and to take on leadership roles in other schools.

A FEW OBSERVATIONS

- Despite very solid and impressive improvements along a wide range of measures — graduation, test scores, attendance, and suspensions — Garcia told me that "no one has ever asked" about any of that. To me, that speaks of the myopia of at least some in the education field who purport to be looking for ways to improve schools and yet ignore the improvement in front of them.

- Improving Artesia wasn't a short-term proposition. It has taken many years of consistent leadership, but that improvement is now embedded in the way every teacher and every school leader works.
- Through an intentional leadership development process that Garcia considers comparable to graduate school, Artesia has helped launch leaders elsewhere in the district and in the wider area.
- The work at Artesia has been supported by a district that provided help and a long-time collaboration with the district union.
- As with other unexpected schools, Artesia has more programs, initiatives, and systems than is possible to put into one chapter of a book. But they all work together in a coherent way to support the basic processes of focusing on what students need to know, collaborating on how to teach it, assessing to see if they've learned it, using data to find patterns and adjust instruction, and developing relationships.
- The systems in place are regularly monitored. If they work to improve student achievement, they are intensified or expanded to reach more students; if they don't work, they are modified or jettisoned.
- All the work, all the systems at Artesia, are animated by a deep belief in the ability of students to reach high academic standards if they have support and help.

CHAPTER TWO

"It's Not Just That"

Systems at Malverne High School, Malverne, New York

On a visit to Malverne High School in Malverne, New York, in the spring of 2016, I told members of the school's leadership team that I was struggling to find a book title that would be simple and convey the complexity of what expert educators do.

Jason Mach, who chairs the district's English, Social Studies, and Library Sciences departments, agreed that the work is complicated but said that the key to Malverne's success was that, "We're not task-driven, we're mission-driven. We're doing this for a reason." What he meant was that adults in the school are committed to ensuring that their students, many of whom might have limited opportunities outside of school, find a way to be successful.

"Yes, but it's not just that," I said, meaning that the commitment of the faculty and staff is only one piece of a complex puzzle of success. Everyone in the room nodded and Mach said, "There's your title: It's Not Just That."

FIRST, THE DATA

Before I start laying out the Puzzle That Is Malverne, I should make the case for why it is important to do so. That is, why do I say Malverne High School is successful and thus worth learning from?

As always, I begin with the data.

Ninety-three percent of Malverne's class of 2015 graduated with a Regents Diploma, which in New York is the regular academic diploma issued by the state. Fifty-four percent earned an advanced designation, which means students succeeded in passing a college preparatory course of study including an additional science class, Algebra II with trigonometry, and three years of a foreign language. Somewhere between 60 and 70 percent of the class of 2016 were on track for an advanced diploma in the spring. To provide a comparison, statewide 78 percent of students graduated, 32 percent with advanced designation.

Malverne's numbers would be fairly ordinary in a white, middle-class school where most students came from college-educated families. But they are highly unusual in schools with demographics similar to Malverne's. About 80 percent of Malverne's students are students of color, mostly African American but with a sizeable number of new immigrants from Central and South America, the Caribbean, and Africa, and 48 percent of Malverne's students qualify for free and reduced-price meals.

FIGURE 2-1
Malverne High School Graduation Rates, 2015

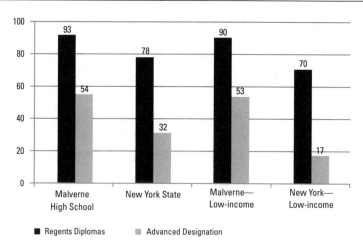

Source: New York State Department of Education
Data shown are four-year cohort grauation rates

Just to provide a little perspective, 65 percent of New York's black or African American students graduate, 13 percent with an advanced designation. The numbers are only a little bit better for students who are designated as economically disadvantaged, 70 percent of whom graduate, 17 percent with an advanced designation. At Malverne, 90 percent of economically disadvantaged students graduated in 2015, 53 percent with advanced designation.

Many of Malverne's students experience considerable struggles. One student arrived in ninth grade as her father was dying and her mother imprisoned. Another arrived in ninth grade after having been placed in a foster family. We'll return to what they said about their high school later, but the point is that Malverne doesn't serve a population of students who are considered, in the education world, to be easy. And it exists in a complicated surrounding context as well.

Malverne's enrollment area includes two towns a few miles east of Queens in Nassau County, which is the western half of Long Island, New York. Those two towns are Malverne, which is mostly white and middle class, and next-door Lakeview, which is mostly African American and working class with a recent influx of immigrants, some very new to the country.

Nassau County is home to the first post-war American suburban development, Levittown, and has experienced many waves of migration from New York City. As a whole it is very diverse but has a long history of racial separation, beginning with Levittown itself. Levittown openly barred African Americans from renting or buying until 1948, when the Supreme Court ruled such housing covenants illegal; but even when it was no longer legal, Levittown informally continued excluding African Americans. Even today Levittown remains overwhelmingly white, and stories of real estate agents "steering" white home buyers to white areas and black home buyers to black areas remain common in Nassau County. A recent Teachers College report led by scholar Amy Stuart Wells said Nassau County is "incredibly diverse in terms of race, ethnicity, and class, but it is also one of the most fragmented, and unequal, counties in the U.S."[1]

All of this means that Malverne High School navigates fraught political waters, with continual levels of distrust that sometimes bubble over. It managed to remain integrated until sometime in the 1990s when most of the white students disappeared into parochial and private schools, leaving its student body almost entirely black.

There is no question that Malverne High School hit a low point in the 1990s. In 2000—the first year New York State reported graduation rates—only 38 percent of students graduated with Regents (New York State–issued) Diplomas, and very few students scored above an 85 on any of the Regents exams, the end-of-course subject exams used in New York.

In contrast, in 2015 more than half of students scored above 85 on the English and US History and Government exams. High scores were less common in other subjects, but high achievement is now a fairly common occurrence. That and the fact that it didn't have significant achievement gaps among groups was the reason Malverne was one of only fourteen schools recognized for its "high progress" by New York State.

In the spring of 2016, the school's salutatorian was admitted to several Ivy League colleges and Stanford University. That was just the icing on the cake, though: 92 percent of the class of 2015 said they were headed to college, 60 percent to four-year colleges.

Quite a few Malverne graduates are able to enter college with college credit. In 2015, 145 students—almost one-quarter of the student body—enrolled in Advanced Placement classes, all of whom took the associated exams. And in 2016, 83 percent of AP students scored a 3 or higher on an AP exam—18 percent higher than the NYS averages and 23 percent higher than the global average.[2] This contrasts with 12 percent passing an AP exam in 2008, when many fewer students were in the classes. In fact, Malverne's success in increasing access and success to AP classes earned the school an invitation to send a team to speak at the College Board's 2016 Dream Deferred Conference on the future of African American education.

Many students at Malverne not only take multiple AP classes but also participate in sports, drama, the band, chorus, and other activities. The robotics team has more than one hundred students. To show how unusual that is, a nearby high school with more than three thousand students had six students on the robotics team.

"I call it Little New York," said Al Lewis, a retired New York City principal whose grandchildren attend Malverne, "because it never sleeps."

Malverne students are involved in so many activities that teachers and administrators have begun to wonder whether they need to encourage students to cut back. "Some of them aren't getting enough sleep," said Assistant Principal Kesha Bascombe, noting that play rehearsals often last until 9 p.m. and some Advanced Placement classes and academic intervention classes are scheduled for "o period," meaning at 7:15 a.m., before school officially starts. When I asked a few seniors if they slept enough, they laughed and said they had trained themselves to get along on four or five hours a night. "It's so easy for us to be involved in everything," said senior Jesse Pace, the valedictorian of the class, who was heading for the honors program at Stony Brook University.

The problem of over scheduling kind of snuck up on Malverne because for a long time the drive among teachers, administrators, and staff was to try to engage students in school. School engagement had begun—like everything else—at a low point. When Dr. Vincent Romano, who is now principal, was chair of the social studies department in 2006, he said the assistant principal asked him to cover the doors during a pep rally. "I didn't know why he asked me that, but I figured a few kids might try to leave— instead 150 kids poured out the back. There was no pep back then, there was no school spirit, and students didn't feel they needed to support their fellow students."

The push to involve students in as many activities as possible is reflected in the fact that teachers and coaches coordinate schedules to make sure that students who are supposed to be in an AP review class don't run into a conflict with a play rehearsal or football practice. "We don't want the students to have to make a choice, so we work out the conflicts," said the chair of the arts department, Michael Messina, who brags about the award-winning chorus and band, both of which have almost more students than can be accommodated in the music rooms.

One more piece of data to show the change at the school: in 1999, 118 students were reported suspended—an extraordinary number for a small high school with an enrollment of less than 600. In 2015, 14 students were suspended.

"We were off-balance" is the way the Joseph Aquino described the school in the past. Aquino is the school's social worker, who has been at Malverne since 1999. "Things were always changing, and it created a culture of uncertainty." Today, he said, "There are consistency and high expectations."

To sum up, not only has Malverne achieved a fairly high level of absolute performance on a number of different measures—graduation, discipline, academics, and student involvement in athletics and extracurricular activities—but it has improved on every one of those measures dramatically.

"A HIDDEN GEM"

A few years ago, once they felt the school was doing well, the staff began referring to Malverne as a "hidden gem" because of its unrecognized success. That success is often overlooked, for example, by teachers in other nearby districts. "We're surrounded by affluent white towns," social studies teacher Brian China said in explanation of that, adding that outside teachers often assume Malverne's teachers are hoping to leave at the first opportunity. English teacher Vincent Toscano, who grew up in the town of Malverne, said that "Malverne [High School] had a bad reputation and the stigma hasn't faded." He is sometimes asked if he had ever been shot at school, to which his response is a surprised—and affronted—"What are you talking about?"

African American students at the school are less surprised by this attitude. Senior Briana Atkins said, "As a person of color, that's something you deal with your whole life." But white teachers seem less inured to the way a primarily African American school is treated—and surprised such treatment continues even when the school performs at levels comparable to many of the surrounding white, high-income schools.

The local community has begun to recognize the school's high performance, however—a recognition marked by a small trickle back of white students, who now make up 15 percent of the student body, and the passage of a school bond in 2011, the first in many years, which superintendent Dr. James Hunderfund considers to be a public vote of approval. The school board approved a bond request that was passed by voters in November of 2016. It will pay to build a new wing of the school that will include science and engineering classrooms.

Malverne High School is far from perfect, and every adult there can tick off failures and disappointments. But it has experienced a success that would be the envy of many other schools, which makes the key question: What makes Malverne as successful as it is?

"IT'S ABOUT THE RELATIONSHIPS"

Romano is the first to say that "there is no magic bullet," but if he is pushed to identify one thing that makes Malverne successful, he says, "It's about the relationships."

Romano began building relationships with students back when he started as an assistant principal in the 2008–2009 school year. The year before, he said, Malverne had the highest rate of suspensions in Nassau County. "If you get rid of kids, what does that do for the kids?" he asks.

This question is a personal one for him. His father, whom he considers to be "the smartest man I know," came from what he described as a very rough upbringing and was kicked out of high school. As a result, Romano said, his father drove a truck his whole adult life. "He could have done something so much more." His father's experience makes Romano think, "A high school that doesn't give up on kids, believes in their potential, and provides them with all of the necessary support and encouragement to succeed can make a lifetime of a difference for a person."

As an assistant principal, he brought that approach to discipline. "Discipline is teaching," he said. "All I did all day long was discipline. It took time. You had to listen. You knew you did a good job when you got thanked for a suspension."

One of the students who gave him a particularly hard time that first year, Dominique Nickerson, returned to Malverne on one of the days I was there. She had come to talk with a class of freshmen students considered at risk of failure.

She told the students that back when she was a freshman she spent a lot of time roaming the hallways, getting in trouble, and being bothered by the fact that "I didn't have anything special to do."

After her freshman year, her family moved and she drifted from school to school, often getting into trouble. She never managed to graduate, but the entire time, she said, she had this "voice in my head" telling her she should be in school and she could be successful. She came back to Malverne to say that she had enrolled in Nassau Community College with the ambition of becoming a teacher.

I asked her: Whose voice was it she kept hearing all those years? The answer: "Mr. Romano's."

I told Romano I thought it extraordinary that his voice had stayed with her. "I spent a lot of time with her," Romano said, laughing. "A lot of time. She gave me a lot of trouble."

Nickerson is a testament to the every kid, every time philosophy at Malverne.

There are many other examples, starting with the class that Nickerson was talking to. The class had started, as so many things at Malverne do, with the data.

"We were looking at our failures and noticing that we were losing students in ninth grade," Romano said. "They might not formally drop out then, but we lost them then." Malverne administrators began working with the middle school to identify the students who were most at risk of failing. They meet with the students and their families during the spring of eighth grade to map out a plan of success and then have them participate in a summer program that include some leadership activities, some service activities like serving meals in a homeless shelter, and some recreational activities, as well as some academic work. "We knew we had to make it fun because we couldn't make them attend," Romano said.

Most students do attend, and that summer experience is followed by a year-long class that has as its purpose keeping the students organized, keeping them on track for homework and tests, and helping them understand how to navigate high school. "The teacher teaches us how the school runs," is the way one student put it. Freshman failure rates are way down, as are dropout rates.

When I visited the class, the students were open about their prior problems. "I got in a lot of trouble," said one about middle school. "Like a lot of trouble. I would yell at a teacher and get thrown out and be in [in-school suspension] all day." As part of this special class, though, he said that he learned that "college people will look at the ninth-grade year," so he has worked to control himself.

It should be noted that freshman failure is a common problem in high schools. Typically, students will start with clean slates from middle school, but by the first marking period, when they start failing classes, they become ineligible for sports and afterschool activities. That begins the long slide of failure and disengagement, which often leads to students dropping out.

"We decided to see if we could stop that before it happened," Romano said.

Here's another example of the kind of system that Malverne puts into place to support students. A few years ago administrators were looking at the discipline data—that is, which students were running into trouble, for what and how many times. What they found was that they really didn't have much of a problem with the boys. "We were having a lot of girl fights," said assistant principal Bascombe. So they set up a club for girls that meets regularly; counselors and other adults help the girls who were getting in the most trouble navigate their feelings and talk through the way they might handle difficult situations. "The GIRLS (Growing Into Respectable Leaders) club has prevented so many fights and Facebook problems," said Bascombe. "That was a big turnaround for us."

Another important system that helped the school get discipline under control, Romano said, was instituting Saturday detentions. A Saturday detention, Romano said, "is stronger than a simple detention and it does not take away from class time. When we suspended kids from school, they often fell behind in their work—then became more of a behavior problem . . . the cycle continues. We also noticed that as instruction improved, so did discipline in the classrooms, but this was a great start to decreasing suspensions."

Sometimes the solutions are even more personal. "We had a kid with some issues settling down," said dean of students, Chris Brescia. "I brought him into the weight room and showed him how to use the weights, getting to know him—and tire him out."

Dealing with all the individual issues started to feel overwhelming to Bascombe. The teachers "don't always have time to talk to every student to know what's going on," she said, "and if I told them that, say, the student's parents were getting divorced or a parent was going to jail, they would say, 'I didn't know.'"

Bascombe saw the need for action. She made sure that every student about whom the school had concerns—which means more than one-quarter of the students—has a plan in place that is mapped out on an Excel sheet, along with the person or team of people who have agreed to be the primary contacts and mentors for that student. Sometimes the plan is football—because the football coach is one of the school's key mentors. Sometimes it is regular counseling with the school social worker. The plan can be an array of activities. But if a teacher has an issue with a student in class, he or she can look at the Excel sheet and know what's being tried and who to speak with to find out more.

"That way there is a system," Bascombe says, "And I'm not just putting out fires."

That seems to be the key to Malverne's success: there is a system.

Knowing that many of their students arrive not ready for advanced academic work, Malverne has a system to get them ready. Knowing that many of their students have little support for academics at home, it has a system to get them support, including an after-school homework club staffed by a certified teacher, peer tutoring, peer mentoring, and lots more. That doesn't mean that all the systems they try work. "We have a long list of things we've tried that didn't work," Romano said. But the focus is always on solving problems for individual students and then building systems that will work for others.

For example, let's return to the two students mentioned earlier—the senior whose father died and mother was incarcerated—Tia Fisher—and the junior who arrived at Malverne as a result of being placed in a nearby foster home. Both were part of a group of students chosen to meet with me because they had all had fairly serious challenges when they first entered Malverne.

Both described themselves as "angry" when they first arrived at Malverne, involving themselves in "drama" and getting in fights. "I was depressed," the junior said, adding that "foster kids often give up really fast." At Malverne, she said, "There was a lot of support. I was able to open up and realize that I don't have to be angry." She found people she could trust at Malverne, naming as one of the most important people the social worker, Joseph Aquino, who spent a great deal of time with her. She is now planning on a career in veterinary medicine.

Tia, who also described herself as continually involved in "drama" when she was a freshman, said that Aquino and the counselors had helped her realize, as she put it, "You have to make yourself stronger." High school chemistry became a turning point for her. She had never had to study much in order to have good grades, but she couldn't simply skate by in chemistry. When her third-quarter report card said she was failing, first she cried. "That's not who I am," she told herself. She buckled down and studied, pulling out a passing grade. Since then she has kept herself focused on her goals and her classes. In the spring of her senior year, she was choosing among several of State University of New York's flagship colleges with the eventual ambition to become a police detective.

Other students have similar kinds of stories. David McAleese, whose passion is video game development, said that when he first arrived at Malverne, "I was happy with 75 and just passing the bar. Last year I realized I have to actually study." He was nationally recognized in SkillsUSA, a technical education competition. Another student said, "I was not serious about school. I was focused on having a social life and drama." Now she is planning on being a nurse practitioner.

Many of the students credited Aquino and the three school counselors for the help they had given. "They are there to help you," Tia said.

"ABOVE AND BEYOND"

That's what Jason Mach had identified—the mission-driven faculty and staff.

Social studies teacher China says the basic motto for teachers is "above and beyond," and students seem to agree.

"The teachers are really devoted to their students," said one senior. Another senior student added, "The teachers are so dedicated to their students they will change their home schedules to help them." Sophomore Olivia St. John agreed. "The teachers want to help you. I can't tell you how many times I've heard the words 'I'll make it work.'"

What this means is that teachers teach extra classes to help students master the material; they hold review sessions on evenings and weekends before the Advanced Placement exams; they are in early to hear about students' problems and late to coach and lead clubs and after-school activities.

"It isn't a job, it's a calling," said one teacher who seemed to speak for them all.

Walking through the school and into classrooms, the teachers seem like the teachers every adult wishes they had had or their kids could have. Knowledgeable about their subjects, they work hard to ensure that their students understand the material. But they all seem to have the same spirit as chemistry teacher Patrick Nolan, who says, "I love science but I love teaching more." By that, he means doing what it takes to help his students learn science—and that means occasionally abandoning the curriculum to build relationships with students. "I know it's a cliché, but it's true—they don't care what you know until they know that you care."

Certainly, students seem to care about what they are learning. They are discussing, asking questions, performing experiments, and explaining results. Teachers are talking, listening, circulating, questioning.

That doesn't mean that any one at Malverne is complacent. Department chairs and administrators are always looking for what more can be done to clarify, engage, and deepen learning, and that can be seen by touring classes with the principal. After sitting in a Spanish class where students were presenting posters to their classmates, Romano said he would have liked to see more engagement among the audience members. "They should have had some role in critiquing the posters." After watching a class where a teacher was experimenting with a "fishbowl" discussion in which three students held a discussion about apartheid in South Africa surrounded by their classmates, he said he was glad to see the teacher trying something new but would have liked to see the students address deeper, more penetrating questions.

This process was repeated in many classrooms. Romano's observations were respectful and deeply appreciative of the knowledge, skill, and experience of the teachers involved. But all were aimed at thinking about how the lessons could have been better, how they could have provided more opportunities for students to learn. The underlying attitude was that even if perfection itself is unattainable, it is always possible to move toward it.

Teachers at Malverne are regularly provided with that kind of feedback on their lessons, but when Romano first began, he said, "There were three years of intense observation." Back then standard instruction in the school was "handouts and textbook reading." It took a long time, he said, before instruction absorbed the principles of "letting kids talk and debate it out. Letting them synthesize and analyze."

This intense administrative focus on core instruction stands in sharp contrast to most high schools. Many teachers rarely see their principals or other administrators in their classrooms. When they do, it is often for quick walk-throughs by administrators armed with checklists of what they want to see. Romano uses the checklists required by New York State when he does formal teacher evaluations, but the core of his work is to help teachers think more deeply about what more they can do to improve, and that requires spending the time necessary to understand their work. At Malverne, each untenured teacher is observed six times a year by Romano, other administrators, and department chairs—a process that involves a preconference, a full-class observation, and a post-conference with specific suggestions on how the teacher could improve. Tenured teachers are observed twice a year.

When teachers are hired, they are told that they will be expected to continually improve. That is after a detailed interview process in which students, parents, and teachers participate along with administrators. This process seems to attract just the kind of teachers Malverne wants— teachers who continually think about how they can do their jobs better.

Not that Malverne hires many teachers any more. In fact, in the spring of 2016, Romano couldn't think of a single vacancy that would need to be filled for the following year. The reason isn't that Malverne's teachers couldn't get jobs—and make more money—elsewhere. Before a contract was ratified in the spring of 2016, the district had gone without a teachers' contract for more than a year-and-a-half, a fact that clearly rankled the teachers. "We're second from the bottom," Nolan said, of teachers' pay in comparison with other Nassau County districts. "We stay because of the kids."

Between 2008—when Hunderfund became superintendent—and 2012, twenty-seven teachers were hired. "We did get rid of a lot of people," Hunderfund said. "And we were very picky about tenuring people." By that, he means that, to be hired for the third year and thus gain a right to due process, teachers must demonstrate a great deal of knowledge, skill, and commitment. This is in contrast to many schools where, if a teacher does nothing particularly wrong, it is common to drift into tenure. But since that big push, Malverne has hired very few teachers.

"A lot of us came in together, and we've all supported one another," said one. "We push each other," said another.

All of this is to say that the faculty is certainly a key component of Malverne's success. But the reason I had said "It's not just that" to Jason Mach is that there are plenty of committed, dedicated teachers in schools that are not successful.

Again, chemistry teacher Nolan provides insight into the role the school plays in the success of teachers. He began his teaching career in the South Bronx in a school where, he said, he "loved the kids to death." But his fellow teachers were so beaten down and discouraged by poor leadership and incoherent systems that they were no longer trying. If he had stayed, he said, he feared he could have been beaten down in a similar way and would never have been as good a teacher as he is today.

"WE WORK HARD BUT WE WORK SMART": THE MASTER SCHEDULE AND OTHER SYSTEMS

The example Malverne provides is not simply one of assembling a staff of committed, knowledgeable teachers who develop good relationships with students, but organizing the work in such a way that helps teachers be successful and stay committed, despite the continual hard work. Social studies teacher China put it this way: "We work hard but we work smart."

Some of that smart work has to do with the support teachers receive, support that goes beyond regular observations. Rose Linda Ricca, assistant superintendent for curriculum and instruction, said that every new teacher is assigned mentors "with specific assignments," meaning, for example, that a mentor might specifically be tasked with helping a new teacher establish classroom routines or develop lesson plans. This is all part of opening up classrooms to improve instruction—and to ensure that students get the benefit of the collective knowledge and expertise of the school. "Failures are our failures," said Romano, adding this caution: "But if you keep it to yourself, they're your failures."

Malverne's support also means that when teachers ask for something, "they get it," in the words of Hunderfund.

For example, if teachers think students need extra AP review classes, the district will find money to pay teachers to stay that extra time. If teachers want to try a new computer program that they think can help students learn specific skills or need books or paper or want to take students on a field trip, the door is open to them. They might have to write an application, but if they can provide a good explanation, the odds are good that their request will be met. And if they provide data afterward that what they tried was successful, that is recognized and thought is given to replicating the practice.

The reason this occurs is that data provides the foundation of decision making at Malverne; this is part of what China meant when he said they work "smart." So, for example, when the third-quarter grades arrived in 2016, the leadership team looked closely at the students most at risk of failing. Almost fifty students were failing several classes, including Earth Science. Romano was considering pulling them out of Earth Science and doubling up on some of the other classes for the rest of the year so that the students would at least have a chance of passing most of their classes instead of failing in multiple classes. Pulling them out of this class would require rejiggering schedules for the fourth quarter and for the following year, because students are required to pass three science classes to graduate in New York. Few high school administrators would even think about making such a disruptive move.

At Malverne, though, the idea is that it is vital to get students used to succeeding, and the adults will do what it takes to provide that opportunity.

This example raises a question that arose in the previous chapter about Artesia: school scheduling. Nowhere are a school's values and priorities more on display than in a school's master schedule.

As in many high schools, building the schedule begins with the school counselors. Malverne has three, all of whom believe that their job is to help students define ambitious goals and then achieve them. And over the years addressing these goals has meant infusing students—some of whom had been discouraged by previous experiences in school—with optimism and stick-to-it-iveness. "We bring the horses to water, open their mouths, and splash it in," is the way counselor Nicole Beauford puts it.

The counselors are all aware of stories like that of assistant superintendent Rose Linda Ricca, who began her career in Malverne as a math teacher in 1987. When she asked a student what he wanted to do after graduation, he said, "Same thing my father does. Collect a check and watch television." She said, "My heart dropped. There's so much out there in the world. The kids then needed a dream."

Today, many fewer kids in Malverne talk that way.

For one thing, the middle school has undergone the same kind of improvement as the high school under the leadership of principal Steven Gilhuley. "When I got here," he said, "only one class took Living Environment and Algebra I. Next year, all eighth graders will take Living Environment and Algebra I." He was talking about two classes that in New York are considered high school classes, but many wealthy, white middle schools offer them to eighth graders they have identified as capable of high school work. By ensuring that all eighth graders take those two high school classes, the middle school is helping ensure that Malverne's students will have room in their high school schedules for advanced work. In this, Malverne contrasts with other school districts that assume only some students are capable of academic achievement and both ration advanced classes and rely on parents to advocate for their children. In the district where his children attend, Gilhuley said, his daughter is in an advanced class "because I knew it existed and asked for it." In Malverne, he added, "We don't wait for parents," he said. "We're the advocates."

Right from the beginning teachers and administrators are talking with students about college and careers and advanced classes. The high school counselors go into eighth-grade classes to talk with students about their course choices. "We talk to them about building a resume in high school," said counselor Donna Bailey, so that they will have choices after graduation.

"We tell them we want them to have the problem of not knowing where to go," said counselor Beauford. She and the other counselors were delighted that many of the seniors in the class of 2016 had been accepted to multiple colleges and had to choose among them.

They have all been at the school long enough that they remain surprised at how embedded into student culture hard work and achievement have become. "I had three kids recommended for AIS (Academic Intervention Services) for Global Studies the other day," Beauford said, referring to an extra-help class that meets at 7:15 a.m. "I was expecting a fight, but they just said, 'Okay, miss.'" Years ago, Romano explained, "No one would come to AIS. We don't deal with that now." As students have started doing better, they have themselves become part of building what he calls a "culture of achievement" and are arriving at the high school asking to take advanced classes.

Even so, counselors stay focused on ensuring that students are taking an ambitious course load. So, for example, Malverne requires that seniors take at least six credits, even if they have fulfilled most of their high school graduation requirements. Where other schools allow and even encourage seniors to work half a day, Malverne counselors encourage seniors to take classes that will get them college credits, such as Advanced Placement classes. In this way, the counselors play what Romano calls a "pivotal role" in building a culture of high expectations.

Once the counselors have gotten all the individual course requests from students, sometime in February, dean of students Christopher Brescia sets about building the master schedule. When he was assistant principal, Romano was responsible for building the master schedule and remembers putting in "thousands of hours" on the schedule to ensure that all students were able to take the classes they needed and wanted. Brescia is just as obsessive about ensuring that "no computer should tell a kid no," he said.

Here's an example of what that means: Romano introduced me to two students who are hoping to be teachers, one a foreign language teacher. These students mentioned to me that they were both taking AP Spanish and AP Italian, and Romano started to laugh. He said that when the administrative team had started thinking about the schedule for 2016, he had told Brescia that the one thing they could bank on was that no one would take both AP Spanish and AP Italian, so they put those classes at the same time. "And then these two came along, and we had to change the whole schedule."

High school students around the country can attest that few schools would take the time and trouble to ensure that their ambitions are taken so into consideration in the building of the master schedule.

The schedule is one of many systems that are in place to reach the goal, as laid out by Hunderfund, to "eliminate failures" and get "every child in a college-level class." Hunderfund points to nearby Jericho and Rockville

Centre, both white, wealthy districts where just about all students take some kind of advanced level class and says that's his aim for Malverne. One plan for the future is to institute the "AP Capstone," a new College Board program in which students are expected to conduct original research and produce a capstone project in their senior year. Hunderfund would have liked to bring the International Baccalaureate program to Malverne, but said the cost was simply prohibitive. AP Capstone is an attempt to bring a similar depth and breadth that IB would have brought.

Romano credits Hunderfund with being the voice that never lets him be complacent or make excuses. As committed as Romano is to ensuring the success of every student, he said that even he will sometimes be tempted to shrug and say, "Well, that's the way it is." Dr. Hunderfund, he said, "never lets me say that. He is always asking what more can we do? He never accepts failure."

This temptation to accept the status quo is another way of acknowledging that the work of educating every student is very difficult, and those directly involved can find it tempting to sometimes give up on helping individual children reach high standards. This is especially true because, as English teacher Toscano says, "Comprehension-wise, the students are low."

The fact that many students still arrive at Malverne unprepared for advanced classes means teachers have to think hard about what they are teaching and what barriers and misunderstandings the students might have. Do students know the necessary vocabulary and background knowledge, or will that have to be filled in during the academic intervention classes or the lunchtime and after-school help? Have students built the stamina necessary to do the work necessary? If not, what is the best way to motivate them so that they can learn for themselves that if they work effectively they will learn and get smarter?

All of this is with the understanding that, as superintendent Hunderfund says, "If it's not done in school, it's not done." That is to say, "we don't have families where they can hire a tutor for their children." In fact, he said, even as students have developed greater sophistication about what they want from an education, "We still have parents who don't see a real value in education. Overcoming that is a hurdle."

To build students' academic confidence, the emphasis in the school is not just on absolute performance but on improvement. "If a student isn't yet passing but they've buckled down and is doing homework, we will recognize that improvement," said assistant principal Bascombe. "You would be amazed at how happy they are getting a certificate. They're proud of being successful."

The idea is that if students start improving and then continue, they will eventually be ready for advanced work. But sometimes even some of Malverne's teachers express concerns about accepting all students in advanced classes. "They have come through a system," Romano says about the teachers. "There were the regular kids, the honors kids, the AP kids. A lot of teachers were the AP kids. We're still fighting the idea that it's the haves and the have-nots."

Still, he added: "I understand they have to blow off some steam, and I'm the one who puts the students in those advanced classes, so I have to listen. When I was teaching, I sometimes felt that too—that my kids were not prepared and shouldn't be in AP classes. But then someone would sit down and tell me what a difference I was making with my students and that would help."

In an e-mail, Romano said:

The idea was to stick to the research about the impact of outstanding teachers. I knew I had them, so the challenge became breaking down the barriers of getting students into AP classes and then helping teachers realize that they did have the potential to make that kind of a difference in a student. That they could take a student that didn't have all the high grades and get them through a college-level course in high school. [Before] students needed a certain GPA, Regents score, and a teacher recommendation. We challenged this idea through what we called a Principal's Probation which allowed students entrance into an AP class based more on motivation. It also meant that students had the option of dropping the class if the work proved too difficult or they were not demonstrating their motivation. Very few students came out and since we began the program between 60 and 70% of the students on probation remained in the class and scored a 3 or higher on an AP exam! Our enrollment numbers in AP are still growing.

This message about student expectations has to be clear and it must be spoken about as often as possible; as much as we praise students, we do the same for teachers. When teachers are holding students to high expectations and we see success—that is celebrated too. I think after years of this many of our teachers think they can walk on water!

The purpose of this explanation is to say that Malverne's success derives from a complex interaction of lots of things that begins with the belief that schools should not create the academic "haves and have-nots," as Romano put it, a careful system that supports students who in other schools might be the have-nots, and continually looking at the evidence to see whether those systems are working. They all add up to what Romano says is "absolutely knowing that you can make a difference."

But all of that raises the question: How did Malverne get that way? It's a complicated story, but I tell at least part of it in the next chapter.

SYSTEMS TO NOTE

- A master schedule that ensures that students are in challenging classes with additional support when they need it.
- A system of careful professional support for teachers to help them improve their instruction.
- A system to ensure that any student who is encountering a personal or academic problem has a plan in place that all teachers can easily learn about.
- A system to ensure that students don't have to choose between activities, classes, and extra help.

A FEW OBSERVATIONS

- At Malverne, students are not left to succeed or fail on their own. They are surrounded by a support system that includes counselors and clinicians, teachers committed to their success, and administrators who take the time to build relationships and systems that ensure that no student falls between the cracks.
- Similarly, teachers are not left to succeed or fail on their own. They are supported by a system that includes fellow teachers who provide

help and encouragement; administrators who continually observe, recognize, and provide feedback; and a district that ensures that they have the supplies and resources they need.

- The school is not left to succeed or fail on its own. It is supported by a district that provides necessary resources; a feeder middle school that works with it to ensure students are aimed at success; and a superintendent who continually monitors success and failure, holding the school accountable for making every student successful.

CHAPTER THREE

How Malverne Became Malverne

*Replicating Expertise at Elmont Memorial
High School, Elmont, New York*

To go from a school where 38 percent of students graduated in 2000 to one where 93 percent of students graduated in 2015, as Malverne High School did, qualifies as what the education world calls a "turnaround." Despite a lot of wild claims, genuine turnarounds are relatively rare.

So how did it happen?

Like any story of school improvement, it is a complex story that involves many strands.

One important strand involves the little-recognized power of a single experienced educator who not only built systems for improvement but who trained a whole cadre of system builders who carry on the work.

To follow this particular strand back to its beginning requires talking about Elmont Memorial High School, which is where Malverne's principal, Dr. Vincent Romano, trained as a student teacher and where he began his career as a teacher.

I first visited Elmont, just outside of Queens, New York, in 2005 when it was being led by Al Harper, and I wrote about it in *It's Being Done*. I had gone to Elmont because it was a working-class, mostly African American school with high performance—high graduation rates and high achievement on Regents exams, the end-of-course exams used in New York. It was an impressive school, and I'll give some data in a minute.

First, I want to recount the exact reason I fell in love with Elmont. On the surface it had nothing to do with the school's high achievement, but anyone who has spent time in high schools will see the connection.

I was talking with the school's leadership team—they call it the cabinet—and I asked how many students were ineligible. I was referring to secondary school policies that say that students are ineligible to play sports or be part of clubs or other activities if they are absent too often or fail two or more classes. The original idea behind those kinds of policies was that drama, band, chess club, and sports shouldn't distract students from their primary role as students. But I had seen many schools where ineligibility policies led to students being cut off from the very activities that, in their minds, made school worth coming to. To me, it seemed that ineligibility policies were—too often—not a helpful kick in the rear but a deadly kick in the head.

At Elmont, I was told, some students were "technically ineligible," but most of them were put on contracts that let them continue activities if they got additional academic help. Students might be having a difficult

FIGURE 3-1
Elmont Memorial High School Graduation Rates, 2015

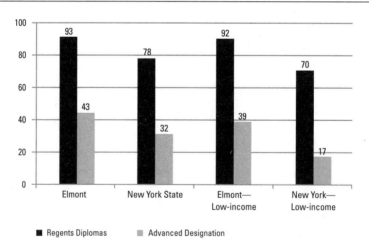

Source: New York State Department of Education
Data shown are four-year cohort grauation rates

time at home and might need the extra support of their fellow students, explained an assistant principal. "We wouldn't want to take that away."

The policy, it seemed to me, was at the same time tough and humane. It kept the emphasis where it should be—on improving academic performance—while honoring the reality that some students might need the lure, support, and connection of their after-school activities. Right then Elmont's big, rather ugly building began to take on human warmth, and I recognized it as a special place.

It took me years to realize it, but I was seeing the influence of an even earlier Elmont leader, Diane Scricca.

I heard the name Diane Scricca on that first visit to Elmont. Many teachers and administrators—including Harper and assistant principal John Capozzi, who gave me a tour of the building—told me, with a note of pride in their voices, that they had been hired and trained by Diane Scricca, who had led Elmont for the thirteen years before Harper became principal in 2002. I made a mental note to try to find and talk with her, but it took years before I was able to.

In the meantime, Harper left Elmont to become superintendent of one of the elementary school districts that fed into Elmont in 2006. I still remember the sinking feeling in my stomach when I heard he was leaving. I knew how a change of leadership could undermine even the strongest school, and I feared for Elmont's future. But then I heard that John Capozzi had been named principal, and I was once again confident that Elmont would move forward.

Let's go back to my first visit to Elmont because it demonstrates something about school improvement. Harper was proud of how successful Elmont was, but he wanted his students to have the opportunity to do real scientific research the way students at nearby, wealthy high schools did. His dream was that Elmont nurture some Intel Science Award winners, and he proudly showed me his new project. It was a tiny classroom—really an oversized office—crowded with Bunsen burners and animal cages that he had turned over to a teacher to begin a science research class.

Ten years later, long after Harper left, his dream was realized when senior Harold Ekeh became an Intel Finalist with research on an aspect of Parkinson's disease and was then admitted to all eight Ivy League colleges.

The following year, 2016, Augusta Uwamanzu-Nna repeated Harold's success with research into a kind of cement that might have prevented the BP oil spill disaster, earning her not only the Intel Finalist status but also an invitation to the White House Science Fair. Admission to all the Ivy League colleges was the icing on the cake.

They weren't the only students who were admitted to highly selective colleges and who conducted impressive scientific research under the guidance of teachers David Spinnato and Michelle Flannery—they were only two of many—but Harold and Augusta became the public face of Elmont's success, a success that had people publicly wondering what was in the water at Elmont.

This success had nothing to do with the water, but it had begun even before Harper's establishment of the science research class.

That class was built on the solid systems that were in place that permitted it to be successful. And those systems had their roots back in 1990, when Scricca became principal of Elmont.

I began hearing the back story of Elmont when I finally tracked Scricca down. She was then superintendent of Riverhead in Eastern Long Island, though that wasn't a long-lived job. It turned out she hated being a superintendent ("too political!"), and she is now an assistant professor of educational leadership at Mercy College and a consultant with schools. She has co-authored two books detailing the way she approaches the job of supporting teachers and principals, and I was honored to write the foreword to the second book.[1]

"THE LOVE OF MY LIFE"

Scricca grew up in Queens in what she describes as a well-to-do Italian family, but none of her grandparents spoke English or graduated from high school. In the 1930s her father attended Stuyvesant High School, one of the most prestigious—and hard to get into—public high schools in New York City. "My father was a Stuyvesant graduate . . . in a time when the Irish were considered drunks and Italians were considered dumb."

Her father went on to run a dry cleaning business, sent his children to parochial schools, and told them he expected them to go to college. Of twenty-six first cousins and many other second cousins, Scricca said, only four went on to any kind of postsecondary institution, making her family typical for Italian Americans at the time.

After getting her bachelor's degree in social studies education from St. John's University in Queens, Scricca entered teaching in the early 1970s. "New York City back then was the premier school system in the country," she says. Although her first department chairman told her she should leave education and "go open a pizza parlor," she said that overall she had excellent mentors and supervisors who helped her become a better teacher. Later they groomed her for leadership by encouraging her to get two master's degrees and, finally, her doctorate—all from St. John's University. They also gave her increasingly complex tasks to complete, beginning with running the lunch program for the school of four thousand students. The lunch aides threatened to go on strike because they didn't believe she—the first woman with the job—could do it. "I said give me a week, and if you still think I can't do it, I will step down." She managed it and went on to tackle even more complex tasks.

In 1990, after having served as social studies supervisor and assistant principal, she became one of many New York City educators who leave "the City" to work on Long Island when she became principal of Elmont Memorial Junior-Senior High School. Elmont became, in her words, "the love of my life."

Elmont, the first town on Long Island east of Queens, is home to the sprawling Belmont racetrack. It had been something of an Irish and Italian enclave, but it was increasingly attracting African American families and new immigrant families from the Caribbean and India and later from Africa and Central and South America. The town was part of a central high school district, Sewanhaka, which served not only Elmont but also four other towns, most of which were white and middle class. In 2009 the newspaper *Newsday* reported that Sewanhaka was the most segregated district on Long Island, with three white schools, one somewhat mixed school, and one mostly black school (Elmont).

Although white families had started to move away from Elmont by the time Scricca arrived, the school was still integrated. The data are not publicly available from New York State, but Scricca remembers: "It was about 40 percent white, 30 percent African American, 15 percent Hispanic, and 15 percent Asian, mostly from the poorer areas of India."

When she arrived, she was told all kinds of good things about the school, but many of those things fell apart upon further examination. For example, she was told that 100 percent of students had passed the Regents Exam in Earth Science. "But then I found out that only a few students took it," she said. Walking through the halls, she saw a pattern fairly typical of diverse schools. With about one thousand seven hundred students, the hallways were mixed but the classes were not. Simply walking by a class, she could tell by the student makeup whether it was a Regents, or college-preparatory, level or advanced class—mostly white students—or if it was a general or remedial class—mostly black students.

Again, the data aren't available from back then, but Scricca's assessment was that the school was "mediocre at best" with a graduation rate of about 80 percent.

One of the first issues she tackled was that of students wandering the hallways, a common problem in high schools. Typically, schools have hall sweeps in which administrators walk the halls sending students to in-school suspension or after-school detention. But Scricca wanted to establish a different tone—she wanted students to understand that they were in school to learn. So she had teachers organize packets of materials, and she mustered every professional in the building who wasn't teaching a class first period. Those who didn't walk through the hallways sending kids to the auditorium stood in the auditorium handing out packets of classwork that students were required to complete.

"The first day we had 180 students," she said. "It was wild. The second day we had 18. After that we never had a problem." With students in classes, Scricca focused on what was going on in those classes. "Poor discipline in a school is always a function of poor instruction," she said. She began with making sure that instruction was "bell-to-bell." Teachers, she said, didn't realize how much time they were losing, but they tended to start five minutes late and ended five minutes early, she said. Adding up all those minutes—ten minutes a day for 180 days—meant they were losing the equivalent of 30 days of instruction over the year. She soon realized, however, that teachers didn't know what to do with all that time. "So we started working on 'Do Nows' and lesson design." Do Nows are activities preparatory to the day's lesson that students begin as soon as they enter the classroom so that no time is wasted. By lesson design, she meant having a clear aim for the lesson, a way to link the lesson to prior knowledge, several ways for students to grapple with the new material, and a way for the teacher to assess which students learned it and should move on and which students didn't and needed additional help.

MASTER SCHEDULES AND EXTRA SUPPORT

Scricca saw that the way the master schedule was built created racial separation, denying African American students the possibility of achieving high academic standards. They were being placed in remedial classes because they were perceived as being less prepared. However, those classes didn't remediate anything; they were traps from which students rarely escaped.

To make the school more equitable, she wanted to eliminate all classes that weren't Regents level or above, but she knew this would require changes in how teachers taught. Teachers were used to teaching each level of student separately. To prepare, she took teams of teachers to visit a nearby school that had successfully eliminated the lower tracks of classes; she led book studies of Jeannie Oakes's book, *Keeping Track: How Schools Structure Inequality*; she showed teachers the data on how little success the remedial classes had had; and she provided professional development in how to engage students at different levels of preparation in the same class. The first year she eliminated the lower tracks in seventh grade and, year by year, worked on up through the grades.

The perception that many of the students were unprepared for advanced classes wasn't simply a perception; for many students, it was a reality. So Scricca didn't simply de-track, which might have led to more failure. She created a master schedule that was designed to prevent failure. In English and math—and later in social studies also—she assigned teachers four sections of the same class, which meant that they had to prepare only one set of lessons. Their fifth class would be for their students who were struggling in those classes. The teachers would try to anticipate what vocabulary and background knowledge might be needed to understand an upcoming lesson and then help students master it beforehand. "A lot of times schools have remedial classes," Scricca said. "They wait until kids are confused and then try and undo that."

The resistance Scricca ran into with this plan came from her superintendent, who told Scricca the teachers weren't working hard enough. He told her to schedule teachers in such a way that they needed to prepare three sets of lessons, an order she ignored. "I ignored him a lot," she says. She probably had more freedom than other principals to flout the superintendent because Elmont had gone through five principals in the six years before her.

Elmont's demographic shifts meant that large numbers of students continually arrived all year, which added new challenges for teachers. "So we started Project Welcome," Scricca said. Although the program was initially funded with a grant, the superintendent eventually agreed to continue funding because it was so successful. On Saturday, new students were required to attend school, where English and social studies teachers alternated weeks with math and science teachers, who were specifically tasked with helping new students prepare for and keep up with their classes.

At the same time Scricca was working on how to engage students and teachers more in the school. "When I came," she said, "most sports were coached by people who didn't work in the school." She wanted teachers who would coach and advise clubs and other activities as well as attend school events so that they could get to know their students outside the classroom. "If you see the kid who is really giving you trouble in class be a star in the school play, it helps you see something more in him." But this took time, "It took me years to get everybody to coach and lead an after-school activity. I had to prove that it was important to the students. That didn't happen in one year. It happened in six years."

"WILL YOU LOVE MY KIDS?"

As teachers left, Scricca used the opportunity of replacing them with teachers she had carefully vetted. She became famous for her question, "Will you love my kids?" She was trying to determine who had the "heart" to teach at Elmont, by which she meant doing what it took to help all students learn to high levels. Her basic position was, "I could always teach someone to teach. I couldn't teach them to love and care for children."

Being hired at Elmont wasn't the end of a process but the beginning. Untenured teachers turned in their lesson plans to department chairs every week and would meet with their chairpeople to go over the plans and find ways to make them better. Although exhausting for teachers and department chairs, this system broke down the usual isolation new teachers often experience. Dana Sotirhos, who went on to become department chair herself, remembers that her chairperson, Alicia Calabrese, "took the time to build professional and personal relationships" with her teachers — in part through that lesson planning process.

In addition, Scricca, one of the assistant principals, or a department chair observed untenured teachers six times a year, with the first time being in the first month of teaching. This was part of a system later formulated in the book Scricca co-authored, *Supportive Supervision: Becoming a Teacher of Teachers*. An observation consisted of a preconference with the teacher, a full-class observation during which the observer wrote notes on everything observed, and a postobservation conference during which the key question was, "What more could you have done to make that lesson better?" Feedback was supposed to include many commendations that had as their purpose to "help teachers see why a practice was effective so they would repeat it." Every observation included one or two recommendations for teachers to improve their practice, on the grounds that no one can work on more than one or two things at a time. Often the recommendation was accompanied by a requirement to observe the way a fellow teacher handled a problem that the teacher was having, whether it was classroom management or setting up an independent or group activity.

Teacher observations were never evaluations, and Scricca is impatient with those who confuse the two. "We really need to clearly delineate the difference between an end-of-year evaluation and an observation," she said in an e-mail. "They are not one and the same. The observation, as professional development, should result in providing opportunities for a teacher to engage in individualized professional development (PD). If they learn to reflect and improve their instructional practices, their end-of-year evaluation should reflect how they respond to their PD."

She followed that up with, "God, this is exhausting!" which she knew I would understand reflected her impatience with teacher evaluation systems that use observations as the basis for evaluations. To confuse those two things, she argues, undermines the ability of school leaders to provide nonevaluative coaching and help to teachers, and thus keeps schools from improving instruction. She considers many of the new evaluation systems that states have put in place, in which observations form the basis of evaluations, as actually harming schools' capacity to improve.

Teachers who are ineffective, she says, are ineffective because "they don't know what to do." As long as they are learning and moving toward being effective, they should be supported. Only when they refuse to try to get better should they be encouraged to leave the profession, she argues.

Back to Elmont—all during Scricca's tenure the school was getting better. Graduation rates rose, Regents exam results improved, and by all accounts students were getting along well. It was named a top high school by *Redbook* Magazine, which at the time had one of the few rankings of high schools. Even so, white families were leaving. "I was there when the last white kids left," says David Bennardo, whom Scricca hired as chair of the social studies department in 1996. "It had nothing to do with the school's results. White flight takes a life of its own—especially on Long Island," he said.

Bennardo, who himself grew up in mostly white Plainview, Long Island, had previously worked in Bethpage, a mostly white suburb, before working at Elmont. He found himself confronted with what were clearly racial reactions of white neighbors and friends when they learned he worked in Elmont. "I would lose my mind with anger if I went to a party and heard, 'When are you getting out?' or 'Elmont's really changed.'"

By then Bennardo had, to use his phrase, drunk Scricca's Kool-Aid; Scricca would brook no talk that African American students were in some way less able or less easy to teach than white students. She insisted it is the job of educators to teach the children in front of them. "If someone said the demographics of Elmont are changing from Irish-Italian to African American, she would say, 'Yeah, they're getting better,'" Bennardo said.

Some teachers were furious at Scricca's refusal to acknowledge that teaching at Elmont posed more challenges now that the school was almost entirely students of color and had a higher percentage of students meeting the qualifications for free and reduced-price meals—up to almost one-quarter of the students.

"One teacher said to me, 'I need her to admit we're not Stuyvesant High School,'" Bennardo said. (Stuyvesant remains one of the most prestigious and hard-to-get-in schools in New York City, and almost all the students are wealthy and white or Asian.) "I told her and she said, 'I know that, but I can't admit it for a second or it will allow excuses to creep in.'"

I asked Scricca what made her so fierce on the subject, and she said, "I just always had a heart for equality. I don't know what influenced me." Then, after a few minutes, she said, "Maybe my religious background affected me. I just knew what I had had and I thought that everyone should have that." And that meant, she said, not only high expectations and careful instruction but a "loving, caring atmosphere. We spent a lot of time loving the kids—listening to their stories, hugging them."

One example: "I remember there was a kid wigging out in the hallway and I brought him in to my office and he was mouthing off at me. I knew what he was doing. I told him that it doesn't matter what he tells me, I know you need me to love you. He was big, burly— 6 foot 2. He had a total meltdown, blubbering."

From then on, she said, "He became a project. I checked in on him; other people checked in on him. It's everyone's job to help a kid assimilate and feel loved."

CONFRONTING A "FAULTY BELIEF SYSTEM"

In November of 1999, Scricca took a team to Harvard's Principals' Center where they worked with Jeff Howard, founder and president of the Efficacy Institute, whose influence on her work she counts as "significant."

I was curious about what could have had such a powerful effect on Scricca, so I called Howard to ask him what he had talked about all those years ago. Based on what I told him about her, he theorized that as a teacher Scricca had been able to have a great effect on her students. "And then she comes to hear me speak and begins to understand the cultural factors that keep other teachers from doing what she was able to do. That principal had the drive and all she needed was a couple of key understandings."

What Howard refers to as "key understandings" have to do with beliefs about intelligence. "The primary limiting factor for most educators is a faulty belief system about the nature and distribution of intelligence," he said. "The belief is deep in American culture, which is that intelligence is innate and unequally distributed." As with so many things, this belief takes on tremendous significance for students of color and students from low-income families, Howard said, but they are not the only students affected.

"Teachers have been putting kids into three groups for years—very smart, sorta smart, and kinda dumb. Teachers understand these groups to be permanent." Howard considers this idea to be at the heart of inequity in schools and has been working for forty years to dispel the myth that intelligence is fixed and innate. "I offer a different belief system that holds that effective effort drives development. People who direct their efforts to learning will learn."

During the time Howard has been working, a great deal of neuroscience has confirmed his basic idea that for most part people get smarter as they work to learn more. Although there may be some aspects of intelligence that are fixed, active engagement with challenging material is now understood to be a key to improving intelligence. Cognitive scientist Dan Willingham has done a great deal to help educators understand the plasticity of brains, how learning changes the way brains function, and how teachers can use some of the insights developed by cognitive science.[2]

Researcher Carol Dweck has added to the public understanding with her term "growth mindset," which holds that basic abilities can be developed through dedication and hard work.[3] Dweck has posited that a growth mindset is in direct opposition to what she calls a "fixed mindset," which holds that you are either a "math person" or a "good writer" or not. This belief has the effect of not only discouraging students from tackling new, difficult work—because it might reveal that they are not smart or good at it—but also discouraging teachers from thinking of new ways to impart material and engage students. After all, if their students are never going to be good at math or science or English, why bother? Either they'll get it, or they won't.

As soon as Dweck's work started appearing in the 1990s, Howard began incorporating it into his work. It was, he says, "completely complementary" to the work he had been doing.

"People talk about low expectations," he said, "but no one talks about where they come from. The problem with education reform is that they tried to change the system without changing the underlying beliefs."

Sixteen years after hearing Howard, Scricca credits him with giving her additional insight and understanding that by "giving kids opportunity, supporting their success, giving them more time to achieve, and believing, without hesitation and with great love, they would succeed and achieve."

Re-armed, Scricca intensified her efforts to make sure teachers had the knowledge and skill to improve their students' learning.

"She had a way of praising people that made you want to earn that praise," said Bennardo, looking back on his experience. "She would put teachers' Regents and Advanced Placement results up on the overhead projector in faculty meetings — and this was before anyone else was posting data — and it made some teachers really angry. But you left wanting your results to be up there."

One decision drew a lot of criticism from experienced teachers, and that was to have relatively new teachers, including social studies teacher John Capozzi — whom she had hired in 1993 — teach Regents level classes. "They said Regents level classes needed experience," Scricca said about many of the teachers. "I said, 'Look what experience got us — a lot of failure.'"

That first year, 90 percent of the students in Capozzi's and the other new teachers' classes passed the Regents exams in their subjects — a much higher percentage than in the past. This despite the fact that the classes included many students who in the past would have been kept out of college preparatory classes because of their prior academic records.

"LIKE AN ISRAELI COMMANDO"

With almost one hundred teachers and many other staff members, Scricca herself could not possibly provide all the feedback she thought teachers needed. Instead, she focused much of her efforts on developing the capacity of the assistant principals and department chairs to provide that feedback.

For example, the leadership team would regularly meet together to view an entire videotaped lesson and simulate a full-class observation. They would take notes just as they would during a regular classroom observation and then that evening write their notes on what they would commend the teacher for and one or two recommendations that the teachers should work on. The next morning they would compare notes and learn what their colleagues recommended. That system of calibration was a form of professional development that helped the leadership team members provide feedback that would be helpful to teachers. In addition, she led book studies and discussions of the latest research.

Just as Scricca was leading book studies and reviews of research for her cabinet, department chairs were leading them for the teachers, who were expected to be experts not only in the content of their courses but also the pedagogy of their content.

Scricca was demanding, in other words, the kind of professional behavior that one might imagine that teachers and leaders at Stuyvesant High School might be expected to engage in. And over the years, she said, teachers saw the point and themselves began carrying the message. "I loved it that people came to school dressed like they worked on Wall Street."

She was hard-charging—Bennardo said she "negotiated like an Israeli commando," and her first superintendent advised her to be "more lady-like" in his annual evaluation of her—but by the time she left, Elmont was getting 350 applicants for every vacancy. The word had gotten around that Elmont was a place where teachers worked very hard—Scricca told prospective teachers that they would work harder than they ever had before—but where they were supported and successful.

Scricca left after thirteen years, she told me, because she was worried she could no longer put in all the time and effort that Elmont demanded. This points to the fact that schools are continually changing enterprises; it isn't possible to simply set up systems and expect them to run themselves. There are new students, new standards, new assessments, new financial conditions. All of these changes require continual monitoring and adjusting. To move the school forward, she felt it was time for someone else to take the leadership. She took a job as assistant superintendent in the nearby Malverne School District.

When Scricca left Elmont, at the end of the 2001–2002 school year, the New York State Department of Education reported a 99 percent graduation rate, with hundreds of students earning the highest scores (above 85) on Regents exams and just about all students going on to two- and four-year colleges and technical school. After nine years as assistant principal, Harper became principal and, after he left to be a superintendent, Capozzi became principal for the next ten years.

SUSTAINING HIGH ACHIEVEMENT

Capozzi's leadership provides yet another window into how high performance can be attained and—perhaps even more telling and important—sustained.

As a high school student—decades after Scricca's father—Capozzi was subjected to the low expectations that in many ways were still typical for Italian American young men. His high school's counselors told him that he should be a house painter. Despite that advice, he went to college at State University of New York Oneonta, and then got a job in the furrier industry, during which he traveled the world and was for a time stationed in Hong Kong.

He didn't find the business world fulfilling and decided to return to do what he wanted to do—teach. He applied for a job teaching social studies at Elmont, where Scricca hired him in 1993. "He had such a heart for children," she remembers.

By 1999 Capozzi had earned the Sewanhaka Central High School District's award for teacher of the year, and Scricca appointed him as a dean, where he became part of the school's leadership team.

When Harper became Elmont's principal, Capozzi served as assistant principal, dealing with many of the school's discipline issues. "The goal of discipline is to change the behavior," Capozzi told me back on my first visit. Although Elmont wasn't plagued with the behavior issues of other, nearby, schools, it had its share of suspensions—257 in 2004. Harper told me that Capozzi handled students in trouble with so much respect and dignity that "I've seen him suspend a student when the student thanks him."

Capozzi had, in other words, been fully immersed in what he and others at Elmont call "the system." He had been the beneficiary of the teacher observation and support, leadership training, and many opportunities to take responsibility for specific projects. Still, he said, "You don't know what this job is until you have it."

Being a principal, "if you do it right," he says, is an all-consuming job, taking not only days and evenings but also weekends. That's true for all schools, but high schools are even more complex, with many evening activities from basketball games to the spring musical and PTSA meetings, which meant that Capozzi's daughters—like Scricca's son before—spent a lot of time at Elmont. In the first couple of years, he talked with Scricca almost every day, asking advice or just talking through a problem. "I had her on speed dial," Capozzi said.

I was lucky enough to visit Elmont many times when Capozzi was principal, and each time I came away with new respect for the depth and breadth of the job he and the other educators at Elmont were doing. Capozzi, true to Scricca's vision, saw the heart of his job being to improve instruction, and some part of every day was spent in classrooms, doing formal or informal observations and meeting with cabinet members to ensure that instruction was at the core of their time. "Even when we're discussing kids," said one of Capozzi's assistant principals, Ed Thomas, during one of my visits, "it always goes back to academics."

It should be noted that keeping this focus on instruction takes enormous discipline and careful development of the leadership of others. The reason is that all schools are home to an enormous number of crises, large and small, that can easily draw the attention of principals from instruction. In many ways schools are like small towns, complete with food service systems, transportation systems, criminal justice systems, and entertainment systems. It is no wonder when principals get distracted from the point of school, which is teaching and learning.

Capozzi didn't get distracted. Like his predecessors, Capozzi approached the job with the urgency of someone who understood that he was running an institution that provided the best opportunity his students had to be able to define and shape their lives for themselves rather than having their lives be defined and shaped by others.

Again, like his predecessors, he was keenly aware of the racism that his students faced. He saw the insults of his athletes on social media and during athletic matches; he heard his students' stories of how they faced disbelief when they went to academic events; and he himself heard comments from other teachers and principals elsewhere on Long Island. Other schools had rifle clubs. Capozzi was asked if he had a "drive-by shooting club." It didn't seem to matter that the school's model United Nations team had won recognition for the "best small delegation" in an international conference in Beijing, China, in 2013. It didn't seem to matter that Elmont's results were comparable to the other, much wealthier, whiter schools in the district and state. He and his students were still subjected to skepticism about their results.

One day when a group of students had gathered in Capozzi's office, I asked them how people they meet explain the high academic achievement of the school, and they said, all together, "They think we're cheating."

One, using words I would have hoped would never be used by a young person, said, "I feel we have to work harder and do better than other students just to get the same respect, because we're African American."

THE NAVIGATION SYSTEM

In 2015, Capozzi's last year as principal, salutatorian and Intel finalist Ekeh chose to go to Yale, and valedictorian Ashley Simon decided to go to MIT. As proud as Capozzi and the rest of the leadership team seemed of them and the other top performing students at Elmont, they seemed even prouder of a senior student who had arrived in seventh grade as a mess. "He was always in my office," Thomas said of the student, remembering that he would consistently get kicked out of class for misbehaving. His home life was chaotic, and his older brother had not done well since dropping out of high school. The student posed a real challenge to Elmont's goal that every student should achieve.

This student became part of the school's Child Studies Team (CST) process, in which teachers, counselors, administrators, and the student and family meet and set goals. "All CSTs are based on academics," said Caron Cox, chair of the counseling department. "Through that we'll find out about personal issues," adding, "Severe discipline issues walk hand-in-hand with learning issues."

Exceptionally tall, the student was a natural for the basketball team, but he was failing most of his classes, making him technically ineligible to participate. As part of the CST, he was put on a contract, which made sure he went for additional help so that he could play basketball. When he expressed an interest in being in the school play, more conditions were put into the contract to permit that. "We kept him really busy," assistant principal Thomas said. The busier he got, the more organized he became and the more he learned. The more he learned, the more he tried to learn. Because of his participation in athletics and drama, he developed relationships with far more students than he otherwise would have, and his fellow students tutored him and helped him keep organized. When he walked the stage at graduation, he received a loud round of affectionate applause from students who knew he had overcome a great deal to graduate. "I told him I'm investing in the restaurant he's going to open," Capozzi told me, clearly bursting with pride that someone who could easily have been lost in almost any other high school had found his way to successfully graduate and go to college.

This story illustrates one of the things Capozzi hadn't realized before he was principal, he said—the centrality of the school's student services office, with counselors, psychologist, and social workers.

"They are the heart of the school," he said. "I really didn't realize it until I sat in this chair." As teacher, dean, and assistant principal, he had been so focused on improving lessons and the relationships teachers had with students that he hadn't realized how important the role of counselors and clinicians was to keeping students focused and on track.

Cox, whom Capozzi hired as chair of the counseling department in 2008, described the role they play as "the navigation system" for the school. "We're not the drivers, we're not the mechanics, but we map the way."

At a basic level, the counselors, like many counselors around the country, hand out course-selection forms to students in English classes and meet with every student in ninth through eleventh grades to choose courses. But unlike in many schools, "We like to take ownership of each student's schedule," Cox said. The counselors enter into the computer the requests but also ensure that students are taking not just the required minimums but what will help them meet their goals. "Counselors have to understand the whole child," Cox said. "For example, if a student wants to be a doctor, he should take all the sciences—but he might also want to write, so he should take a creative writing class."

Signing up for courses is just the beginning of the building of the master schedule, which is put together by assistant principal Brian Burke. He spends a great deal of time resolving conflicts so that students don't have to choose between classes they need and want and so that they have a good working schedule the first day of class.

These systems have been finely honed over the years, but they are never immune to change. As Cox said, when she arrived, "there were plenty of systems. Some worked well, some didn't." Cox set to work figuring out which were which, jettisoning or improving those that didn't work and putting in place new ones.

"I can't say one cup of flour and two pinches of sugar and it's done," Cox said. Processes change as the need changes. Ultimately, she said, it's about "the team," meaning the teachers and administrators who are able to assess the success and failure of the systems in place and suggest ways to change.

During Capozzi's tenure quite a few things about Elmont changed. For one, the percentage of students on free or reduced-price meals grew from about 25 percent to about 45 percent, partly a reflection of the severe downturn in the economy in 2008.

That kind of change can be difficult for schools to absorb, but throughout Capozzi's tenure Elmont maintained graduation rates in the 90 percents with a more or less steady increase in the percent of students earning an advanced designation on their diploma.

Scricca, Harper, and Capozzi each brought very different personalities to the job, but each one was clear that all children can learn and it is up to the adults in the schools to ensure that they do. "Your focus is the same," Capozzi said. "But your style is different." They each saw their role as principal as setting up the systems necessary to live up to that promise. Scricca put in place systems to improve instruction, Harper expanded student opportunities, and Capozzi continued and refined all the systems to support students and instruction. "You're never done," Capozzi said. "If you think you've arrived, it's time to leave."

"IT'S ALL IN A DAY'S WORK"

Capozzi didn't think Elmont had "arrived," in the sense that he still saw areas of improvement that should be made, but after ten years he, too, decided he had done what he could and it was time to leave. He was tired—and his wife was tired of rarely seeing him. Once again, this underlines the point that the job of principal, when done right, is big and time consuming.

The things that wore him out most were not the things that went on in the school. For the most part he was energized by his relationships with teachers and students, a cadre of whom would regularly hang out in his office. What exhausted him was, rather, some of the outside pressures. The state had instituted a tax cap that had limited funds, meaning that Elmont couldn't replace some of the teachers who retired or left, and he had had to cut some teaching assistant positions. In addition the new teacher evaluation system that the state put in place in many ways forced him to radically change the observation process that he and others credited with Elmont's success.

"I don't feel I'm an instructional leader anymore," he said, discouraged.

Knowing it would be his final graduation as principal, I went to the graduation in the spring of 2015 and I saw Capozzi tell his students:

> As you move forward the sad reality is that you . . . will face racism and stereotypes. Do not allow these evils to deter you from your dreams and goals. Instead, use your educational foundation to counter the ignorance that unfortunately still exists today. As Nelson Mandela said, "Education is the most powerful weapon which you can use to change the world."

Afterward, he was greeted like a rock star by graduates and their relatives asking to take pictures with him and thanking him for all his work and day-to-day commitment to the students. He says what he did was not all that extraordinary. "It's all in a day's work." But the students and their parents knew that not all educators have the commitment and drive—and know-how—to ensure that all students achieve.

Capozzi began work as assistant superintendent of personnel and administration in the Sewanhaka Central High School District in the fall of 2015. At first he deeply missed Elmont, but after a while, he said, he began "enjoying thinking about education from a different level." He saw his role as one of support of the five principals in the district. If they needed a one-on-one aide for a student with disabilities or a new technology teacher, it was his office's role to help provide that.

That, too, is a mark of the "Scricca System." Scricca, and many of the people with whom she worked, see the school principal as being the key agent of change and school improvement. It is the role of the district, they say, to support principals.

This way of thinking is different from many who work in central districts, who think of principals as middle managers who carry out district policies.

With Capozzi joining the ranks of district administration, Scricca can count at least three assistant superintendents, two superintendents, and nine current principals scattered across Long Island whom she had hired and trained. Bennardo, the former social studies chairperson she hired in 1996, for example, went on to become a principal and is now superintendent of South Huntington School District. His district is experiencing a demographic shift from all-white to one in which about half the students are students of color and students from low-income families. In 2015 its graduation rate was 92 percent.

MALVERNE HIGH SCHOOL AND THE "DIANE SCRICCA BOOT CAMP"

We started with Malverne High School's improvement story, so let's pick back up with Scricca. When she left Elmont, she became assistant superintendent of the four-school Malverne Union Free School District, a job she held from 2003 to 2007. In that role, she was in charge of curriculum, hiring, and professional development.

One of Scricca's key hires at Malverne was Vincent Romano. Romano had grown up in the almost all-white Long Island town of Bethpage, where David Bennardo was his social studies teacher and coach. When Romano first went to college at Stonybrook University, his ambition was to open a restaurant and bar. But Bennardo's enthusiasm for coaching and teaching convinced him to get his teaching degree. "He made you feel smarter, he made you feel bigger. He knows how to build a family," Romano says about Bennardo, adding, "The coaching mentality is very important."

While Romano was in college, Scricca hired Bennardo as chair of Elmont's social studies department, and Bennardo helped Romano do his student teaching at Elmont. "It was so much work," Romano remembers. "I would plan lessons and be observed and have to think about what I could have done to improve those lessons—because at Elmont, student teachers are considered students who need instruction and feedback. It was exhausting. I didn't know if I could keep going."

He did keep going, and when an opening came up, he was hired as a social studies teacher. "I learned how to be a teacher there," he said. "Diane Scricca, Dave Bennardo, John Capozzi—they all had a huge influence on me."

Of Romano, Scricca said in an e-mail, "He grew as a teacher in Elmont, embracing the culture and professional development. He took to leadership training as he did teacher training (great teachers make great leaders), but most importantly, he loves the kids and really believes that every kid can achieve at a very high level. . . . He is the REAL DEAL and then some."

When Scricca went to Malverne, she lured Romano away from Elmont to head up social studies for the district. As in many small districts, administrators wear multiple hats, and the Malverne district doesn't have high school department chairs but district department chairs. Romano's new position meant that for the second time he was working for Scricca. "I say I did two tours," he said, using a term usually associated with military service, with its implication of rigor and demand.

Scricca saw her job as deputy superintendent as being one of helping school leaders develop their skill in improving classroom instruction. With a deep belief that teachers have to "crawl before they can walk and walk before they can run," she talked with leaders about helping new teachers with classroom management, creating a good aim and structure for a lesson, and about engaging students and developing good relationships with them. More seasoned teachers needed to learn about how they might improve their questioning techniques, ensure smooth transitions between activities, provide expert feedback to students, and commit more deeply to the school. By a deeper commitment, she meant leading a club, sport, or activity so that teachers would get to know students at a different level and provide them with more ways to engage with the school.

"We all went through the Diane Scricca Boot Camp," Romano said about the leadership team currently working at Malverne. Even though she left Malverne in 2007, in 2016 it was still possible to hear the sentence "I was trained by Diane" said with the same note of pride that I had heard years before at Elmont.

Eventually, Romano became an assistant principal, first at the middle school and then, in 2008, at the high school. Replacing him in the middle school was Steven Gilhuley, who—like Romano—had been coached in high school and recruited as a brand-new teacher to Elmont by Bennardo. Gilhuley is now principal of the middle school, and he, too, has brought the Elmont sensibility that the job of educators is to "give kids more opportunities," as he puts it.

Here, another strand in the Malverne story needs to be woven in. When Romano went to the high school as assistant principal, it was to work with a principal, Jim Brown, who had taken the job on an interim basis. From Brown, Romano learned a good deal, because Brown had arrived the year after the high school had the highest rate of suspensions in Nassau County and it could be said to have been in crisis. I called Brown to get his perspective on Malverne's improvement, and he said he had come in to manage chaos. "The school was disorganized," Brown told me. "The kids pretty much had their way and the morale of the teachers—you can imagine."

A retired principal with decades of experience, Brown wasn't daunted by the disorganization. He had grown up one of eleven children in a Georgia sharecropper family and played basketball for the U.S. Army and Hofstra University before starting his career as a teacher. He began at Roosevelt High School in Long Island's Hempstead, a school that was so unsuccessful for so long that it became the first school in New York to be taken over by the state. Fed up after seven years, Brown left for nearby Freeport, where he had what he called "a successful career" as a principal for many years.

Brown was called up out of retirement for the Malverne job, and when he arrived, he said, he was focused on providing consistency and high expectations. "The whole point is to create the culture and climate for learning—especially for those students who don't get that at home," he said, adding that he initially focused on discipline. "I started with the students because if you start with the teachers they feel put upon."

Romano became assistant principal in Brown's second year, and Romano said he was very lucky in having Brown's leadership. "He let me take on projects and gave me leeway," he said. Brown in turn said he was lucky to have Romano. "He would always take the ball and run." Brown consciously groomed Romano to be principal, and when the superintendent consulted him, he strongly recommended that Romano succeed him. One of the issues was whether Malverne, with its mostly African American student body, needed an African American principal—something greatly desired by some in the community. "I told [the superintendent], 'You would be doing the black students a disservice if you didn't give the best person the job,'" Brown, himself African American, said.

Now, he says, "I feel like a proud father. Vinnie is doing such a good job making the students successful."

A WINDOW ONTO A KNOTTY QUESTION

Elmont and Malverne provide a window onto one way of thinking about a knotty question that has plagued the education world, which is: How do we not only improve schools but also sustain that improvement and scale it up?

One educator who herself had been the repository of a great deal of training, education, and mentoring has provided systematic training and mentoring to a whole series of leaders—who in turn have done the same. When I told Scricca that I have heard, over and over, the pride in people's voices when they tell me that they were hired and trained by her, she responded, "And people will be saying that about Dave Bennardo, Al Harper, John Capozzi, Vinnie Romano, and Steve Gilhuley. They are now building their legacies."

Scricca, however, was not the only experienced leader who affected Malverne: Superintendent James Hunderfund has brought a lifetime's experience to bear with his impatience with any kind of failure. Similarly, former principal Jim Brown's calm consistency and high expectations helped launch Romano's principalship.

All three represent the ways in which educational expertise has been built and deployed for the benefit of students.

To some, this process might seem slow. Elmont and Malverne certainly do not represent a quick, easy fix. What they do represent, however, is a story of educators—how they develop their knowledge and beliefs, how they learn to shape institutional systems to serve all students, and how they spread that knowledge.

SYSTEMS TO NOTE

- A master schedule that ensured that all students were in college-preparatory or advanced classes, with time built into the day to provide additional support to those students who needed vocabulary and background knowledge previewed before lessons.
- A system to observe and provide support to teachers.
- A system to provide additional support to new students on Saturdays.
- A system to cultivate and develop leaders who go on not only to lead the school but also to lead schools and districts throughout the area, providing a possible model for continuity and replication.

A FEW OBSERVATIONS

- Educators who understand the systems that shape the work of schools can be powerful purveyors of the knowledge and expertise needed.
- True school "turnaround" is not a quick process; it takes time and an enormous amount of work.
- That work requires a deep belief in the capacity of students to learn at high levels.
- Most of my observations from Elmont and Malverne lead to hope and optimism. But it is impossible to ignore the fact that the successes of two mostly African American schools are greeted with as much hostility and out-and-out racism as they are. To those who still doubt that African American students can be successful, I just have to ask: What would it take for you to change your minds?

CHAPTER FOUR

Starting from Scratch

Dr. Robert W. Gilliard Elementary School, Mobile, Alabama

Whenever I walk into a high performing school, I always want to know how it got that way. But I am always aware that no matter how good the memory of the people involved, it's not the same as talking with people as they are going through the process of school improvement.

For many years I have wanted to follow the process of school improvement as it happened. But to say that is a risky enterprise is an understatement. Identifying a school at the beginning of an improvement process is comparable to identifying a Kentucky Derby winner from a new crop of foals two years before. You can pick a foal with great prospects and then it breaks its leg or the trainers don't know what they are doing, or—well, a million different things could happen, and you no longer have a story of promise and success but loss and failure.

My first venture into following a school right from the beginning of an improvement process, back in 2006, will give an idea of what I mean. I was acquainted with the chief academic officer of a large city who was interested in helping me find and learn from success. He told me about a principal he had hired from another state to take over a very low performing elementary school that had been struggling for many years.

Both of them were serious people, intent on improving the education of students in struggling schools, and I thought it would be instructive

83

to follow the process both from the point of view of the school and the district. I visited the school shortly after the new principal arrived, and he welcomed me to his office. The school was a somewhat typical old-style big, hulking, brick building in a hard-luck neighborhood. The principal told me that the day he walked into the building for the first time and saw how sad and dirty it was, he walked upstairs to the principal's office "and I sat down and cried."

He had uprooted himself for this job and, although he was an experienced principal, he had never been in quite such a dysfunctional school. Even so, he was intent on improving it.

He knew that a powerful lever of improvement was for teachers to work together to improve instruction. The first step was for teachers to get to know each other as professionals. A couple of months into school he organized the school's first-ever "walk-through," a group of fifth-grade teachers who visited a handful of classrooms in other grades. I tagged along, and it was eye-opening for me to see just how isolated the teachers had been up until then. Although they had all been there at least one year, and a couple longer than that, none of them had ever been in any classrooms other than their own and maybe that of a buddy.

Most of the classrooms we saw fell into the realm of ordinary school: there was some kind of instruction going on, though it wasn't always clear exactly what students were supposed to be learning or doing. One classroom, however, was startling. For one thing, it was roasting; the radiators must have been cranked up full blast, because it was much hotter than any other place in the school. Even so, the teacher was wearing heavy clothes, gloves, and a coat. Closed blinds added to the oven-like atmosphere. Meanwhile, for the entire ten or twelve minutes we were in the classroom, the teacher was handing out textbooks. To this day I can't figure out how she was able to extend that activity for so long, but she managed. Even with the principal in the room, the class was barely in control. Students were talking and throwing paper and otherwise annoying each other, probably out of sheer boredom. Sitting among the students was an adult taking notes. I later ran into her at a meeting at the district office, and she told me that she was an instructional coach who had been asked to observe the teacher. I suspected, though I never confirmed it, that the principal had asked for the district to observe the teacher preparatory to trying to fire her. The district observer told me she had never seen so little instruction in a classroom, and she confirmed that when the principal was out of the room, the students were completely out of control.

After the walk-through the principal led a debrief of the teachers, and what struck me was that they had no professional language to describe what they had seen. None wanted to seem to criticize another teacher, so they tried to find nice things to say about every classroom, saying things like, "the kids seemed to like her" or "she was trying hard."

Seeing the teachers flounder, the principal eventually modeled conversation about whether classes were focused on standards, what teaching strategies the teachers were using, what evidence of student engagement they saw, and whether any student work was displayed and, if so, what evidence it demonstrated of whether students were meeting state standards. Even he was a bit at a loss to discuss the roasting classroom, but he managed to keep it professional.

I was impressed with the approach the principal was taking to open up instruction to scrutiny and develop a common professional language. I made a couple of other visits to the school where I saw a few attempts at setting up regular systems to handle discipline, involve and inform parents, and improve instruction. But my work took me elsewhere, and I lost touch for a while. When I was able to turn my attention back to the school, I learned that the principal had left to take a job with a charter school and the chief academic officer had become superintendent in another city. All these years later, the school is still a mess with hardly any students meeting state standards.

I had known it was risky to try to watch school improvement from the beginning and chalked that up to experience. The next time I attempted it was six years later, and I had firmer grounds for expecting success. After finishing *Getting It Done,* the book I co-authored on school leaders of unexpected schools, I realized that a number of the leaders we had written about were taking on new challenges as principals of low performing schools. These were proven leaders who had already led high performing or rapidly improving schools with large populations of students of color or students living in poverty. I was confident they knew what they were doing, so I asked a number of them if I could observe them at work. I visited as often as I could, which wasn't as often as I would have liked.

Each visit, however, provided insight into how expert school leaders think about school improvement and what kinds of systems they put into place.

One principal was Debbie Bolden, whom I first encountered as the assistant principal of George Hall Elementary in Mobile, Alabama, and was part of the study of leaders in *Getting It Done*. She subsequently became principal of Dr. Robert W. Gilliard Elementary in Mobile and, as I write this book, she is preparing to take a new job in a different school district, in part so that she can be closer to her aging parents.

THE BACK STORY: GEORGE HALL ELEMENTARY

First, let me fill in a little background. Just as it was impossible to talk about Malverne High School's improvement without talking about Elmont, it is impossible to talk about Debbie Bolden without talking about George Hall Elementary School.

After graduating from University of South Alabama, Bolden began her career as an elementary school physical education teacher in West Mobile, which is the wealthy part of the city. She went on to earn a master's and certification in leadership at University of Alabama where, she told me, "They had a great leadership program." She became assistant principal at Maryvale Elementary School in Mobile, Alabama, where most of the students were African American and most came from low-income families. The principal there was Terri Tomlinson, with whom Bolden had taught in the past. While they were there, Maryvale was regularly honored for its high achievement. Looking back on that experience from the vantage point of time, Tomlinson and Bolden both said that they could see that they had taken a relatively strong school and helped make it better. Their next experience was quite different.

At George Hall Elementary School, just about all the students were African American and from low-income families, and performance in the school was far below any other schools. For many years Alabama gave the nationally norm-referenced SAT-10 test to its elementary school students, and it showed that George Hall's students were reading and doing math at levels far below that of other African American students in Alabama—which means they were performing toward the bottom of the country.

When the state made noises about possibly taking over the school, Mobile took action and reconstituted the school in the summer of 2004. The district appointed Terri Tomlinson as principal and allowed her to bring Debbie Bolden as her assistant principal. Reconstitution meant that all staff members had to reapply for their jobs. Tomlinson had complete discretion over whom to rehire, and she rehired only one cafeteria worker and one building service worker. Everyone else was absorbed into jobs elsewhere in the district.

None of these changes went over well in the neighborhood. The outside world might not have thought much of George Hall, but it was in many ways a treasured community institution. It served an isolated neighborhood, Maysville, which included two federal housing projects, and teachers at the school had taught the parents and even grandparents of children in the school. There was little community trust that these two new white women would care about George Hall's children. Someone hung a cat on the playground, and the building was "fished," meaning dead fish were rubbed on the building. When Tomlinson and Bolden walked into the school that summer, the stench was overwhelming. The inside of the school was no better because the departing staff had trashed the building.

Despite all that, Tomlinson told me years later, "I knew achievement wouldn't be a problem once we put the systems in place."

Tomlinson and Bolden pretty much started from scratch, beginning with making the building a clean, welcoming place ready for teaching and learning. They worked with the one remaining maintenance person to power wash the building, rid the building of trash, reorganize the furniture, and install bulletin boards. "Some days we were too tired to even say good night; we'd just look at each other, get in our cars, and go home," Tomlinson said.

They interviewed potential staff members outside the building because they refused to let any teachers see the building before it was ready. Tomlinson had spent a career in Mobile and had relationships with many teachers, which proved to be a boon for recruitment. Although teachers received an extra bonus for going to George Hall for the first couple of years, that didn't seem to be the draw. "I'd teach anywhere for Terri Tomlinson," one teacher told me. Initially, Tomlinson was not able to attract

African American teachers to the school, which she attributed to the fact that Maysville was notoriously unsafe. The husbands of African American teachers put their feet down and refused to let their wives work there, whereas white husbands were less savvy and didn't realize what their wives were walking into. That, at least, was her theory. After a few years, when the school was more successful, she was able to attract some African American teachers. But that took a while.

Once the building was ready and the staff hired, Tomlinson and Bolden turned their attention to meeting with community members and writing the school handbook, which laid out such basics as behavioral expectations and how students would enter in the morning and leave in the afternoon. School dismissal posed a particular problem because the school's immediate neighbors complained that students had been trashing their yards on their way out of school. Tomlinson promised the neighbors that staff members would walk students home. That began a George Hall tradition.

The first year, with the building clean and organized and the children expected to behave and learn, a visitor from a state education organization who had been to George Hall many times before wondered aloud if these were different children. They were calmer, and the atmosphere was one of learning. "They were even cleaner," she told me, a testament to the fact that the school had bought extra school uniforms and installed a washer and dryer to make sure students could wear clean clothes.

Tomlinson had a big ambition: "to end intergenerational poverty" for her students. But that didn't mean she was naïve about how far her students had to go. Like many students who live in poverty, her students arrived with very little in the way of vocabulary and background knowledge. "Sometimes we have to start by teaching the students their names," Tomlinson told me. "They're so used to being called 'Little Man' that they don't know their names." One teacher summed it up as, "They hardly ever leave their neighborhood. They live ten minutes from the bayou, and they've never seen a boat."

Early on the teachers proposed taking students on field trips to widen their knowledge of the world. Tomlinson was initially doubtful, knowing that field trips can be a colossal waste of time when done badly. She asked the teachers to submit a proposal, complete with what teachers expected their students to learn and do as a result of field trips. They did, the first couple of field trips were completed, and teachers were able to document that students had learned new vocabulary and incorporated that new learning into their writing and speaking. From then on most students went on a field trip once a month, including boat trips, visits to the zoo, and tours of the state capital, among other places—trips that were documented with student videos and essays.

During the first few years, academic achievement as measured by the SAT-10 improved most years. By 2009, the first year I visited, George Hall was one of the top schools in Alabama.

That year I happened to go during its "literacy fair," which to me demonstrated the kind of learning that is possible in an elementary school. Tomlinson told me that the literacy fair had several origins. For one, she thought history had been unduly underemphasized in elementary school curricula. She also hated the way many schools closed up instructionally after state tests had been administered. And she wanted to make sure her students got a great deal of practice writing. All those things were put together in the spring literacy fair, which was spearheaded by the school's writing coach, Melissa Mitchell, who later succeeded Tomlinson as principal.

Snaking through the corridors was a timeline beginning with the first European discovery of the Americas. On the right were murals and illustrations of events—Paul Revere's ride, the March on Washington, the first moonwalk—and on the left side were essays. Students stood in the hallways ready to declaim a poem or read a play about Harriet Tubman or Abraham Lincoln to parents or community members who attended.

That literacy fair was the culmination of huge amounts of work on the part of both students and teachers, and I managed to arrange my schedule so that I saw two more literacy fairs in subsequent years. One time the emphasis was on the 1940s and 1950s; World War II, the Holocaust, and the early Civil Rights Movement were all topics explored in greater depth. World War II veterans came to the school to speak to the upper grades about their experiences. Essays about Anne Frank allowed students to express anger that anyone thought they had the right to kill other people because of their religion; and others about the 1954 *Brown v. Board of*

Education decision let them explain the legal implications of the Supreme Court ruling. I found it particularly poignant to be standing in an all-black low-income school reading student essays celebrating the students' legal right to attend desegregated schools.

Another year the school switched the focus to science, and students wrote about and represented elementary-school-level physiology, astronomy, meteorology, botany, and.biology. In all cases, the work was arranged in such a way that the grade levels were interspersed with each other. That way, fifth graders could see how far they had progressed from kindergarten paragraphs, and kindergarteners could see what lay before them in longer, more organized and knowledge-filled fifth-grade essays.

By the time I got there, George Hall was one of the top performing schools in Alabama. Tomlinson told me that one of the keys to their success was that "we never blame the kids. In fact, we try not to place any blame in this building. What we do is look for solutions," she said. "The kids can't help what they come from. It's up to us to figure out the ways to teach them."

Tomlinson told me that she didn't understand what the wealthy white schools that weren't performing at such levels were doing. "I think they're coasting," she said to me. That is to say, because their students entered with so much social capital, the schools didn't have to think about reorganizing themselves to get the maximum possible effect from their efforts. The students of George Hall permitted no such complacency. If they were to meet any kind of recognized academic standards, George Hall would have to operate at maximum efficiency. She said she had no doubt that if schools with more social capital operated the way George Hall did, their achievement would be off the charts.

In 2011, the last year Alabama administered the SAT-10, George Hall's students scored near the top of the nation; that is to say, fifth-grade students at George Hall were at the eighty-eighth percentile in reading, meaning that on average they were reading better than 88 percent of fifth graders in the nation. That same year they were awarded the Intel award for their math achievement.

All that is by way of giving a sense of the experience Debbie Bolden had. She had been part of a team that more or less built George Hall from the ground up—what the current principal, Melissa Mitchell, calls The

Transformation. As Bolden put it, she spent "two rough years and three great ones" at George Hall.

"HELLHOLE"

I was aware that Bolden had left to become principal of another school in the 2009–2010 school year, but I hadn't focused on the fact until I saw her at George Hall's literacy fair in the spring of 2011, leading a team of her teachers through the hallway. She wanted them to see the level of work their students were capable of. She later told me that mostly the teachers had told her such work would be impossible at Gilliard. "They kept saying they didn't have time to teach social studies," Bolden told me, shaking her head.

In 2012 I asked if I could visit to witness the changes Bolden was bringing to Gilliard, and she agreed. So I didn't visit until she was in her third school year as principal, but the beginning was still very fresh in her mind and the minds of many of the teachers and staff. "This was the filthiest, dirtiest school I had ever seen," Bolden told me. "The only difference with George Hall was that the staff hadn't trashed it." The previous principal told her, "I hope you can get the custodian to work, because I never was able to."

Dr. Robert W. Gilliard Elementary School is a much newer building than George Hall, built to combine two smaller elementary schools. In 2012 it had about 700 students, and by 2016 it had more than 800, 97 percent of whom qualify for free and reduced-price meals. The building is all one level and somewhat maze-like, which makes it a little difficult to keep tabs on.

One of the first questions Bolden was asked when she arrived was who she wanted on her "restraint" team. She didn't even know what was meant by that term, but it turned out that in the past teams of teachers and staff members would regularly be called into classrooms to physically restrain an out-of-control child. She responded that there would be no need for a restraint team, a statement that was met with skepticism. After all, students at Gilliard were angry and regularly acted out. For that matter, parents were pretty angry too and were used to roaming the halls. "Getting the kids in line wasn't a problem." Bolden said, although that first year she was there, she had 469 suspensions. The biggest challenge, she said, "was building relationships with the community."

Unlike at George Hall, Bolden said, most of the Gilliard parents had jobs, often low-paid jobs such as in fast-food restaurants. Though Bolden estimated that about two-thirds of parents had graduated from high school, few had any college. "Many had bad experiences in school," Bolden said. At George Hall, she said, "Once parents saw we weren't scared to go in their home and once they knew we cared, they were on our side. Our parents [at Gilliard] are more educated and are consistently more resistant."

In the 2008–2009 school year, the year before Bolden arrived, the SAT-10 results were that Gilliard's fifth graders were at the thirty-ninth percentile and forty-fifth percentile in reading and math, respectively, meaning they were, on average, scoring above 39 and 45 percent of other fifth graders in the country. The school had officially been put "on improvement" by the state.

"Hellhole," said Bolden. "That's what all of Mobile called it. The superintendent told me it was the worst staff ever assembled in Mobile."

First-grade teacher Deborah Sizemore confirmed that, though with less colorful language. She had come to Gilliard initially as a reading coach under the old principal. "I really believed I could make a difference," she said. She had had a great deal of training in early reading instruction as part of Alabama Reading Initiative, a statewide program to improve reading instruction, that she was eager to share with Gilliard's teachers. But, she said, her efforts were pretty much stymied by the way the school was organized. "They had no routines in place and no expectations for children," she said. In addition, there was no system—no common planning time and no professional development time—during which she could work with teachers to increase their knowledge of reading instruction, which is what her training had prepared her to do. She was left to simply work with individual teachers who agreed to work with her, and only a few did.

As an example of what she found, kindergarten students didn't learn their letters and sounds, Sizemore said, a fact that the kindergarten teachers excused by saying their classes of about twenty-five students were too big. "Excuses are just what they say not to do their job." Frustrated at her inability to bring schoolwide change, she retreated to teach in a first-grade classroom where she could at least make sure some students learned to read. Bolden told me about Sizemore: "She takes the lowest of the low and makes sure they read. She accepts no excuses." Sizemore was one of those who welcomed Bolden's arrival, but many others didn't.

The assistant principal, for example, wrote Bolden an angry e-mail saying she should have been made principal instead of Bolden. The assistant principal transferred, but most of the teachers stayed. Bolden said she thought the teachers were trying to wait her out.

Bolden asked the district if she could choose her assistant principal and was told no. "I just wanted one person I knew," she said. The assistant principal assigned by the district was initially on maternity leave. When Metra Turner did arrive, Bolden considered herself lucky: they were a good match and Turner worked hard. Initially, she said, "I had no one." This was a huge difference from George Hall, where "we all went in there together."

Turner confirmed Bolden's description of Gilliard back then. "Before I came here, I always heard it was a zoo. And it was," she said. She was stunned to find that kids were so unruly that there were "beatdowns in classes. . . . I've never worked with a staff with this lack of work ethic."

The summer Bolden arrived she first turned her attention to the building, bringing in the maintenance staff from George Hall to help over the summer to get it into shape for the arrival of students. "I went through four custodians," she said, before she found someone who would take responsibility for having a clean building.

She also reassigned classrooms. The previous principal, she said, had let some teachers choose their classrooms, and they were somewhat helter-skelter. Bolden wanted all the teachers on a grade level to be near each other to better facilitate collaboration and the kind of camaraderie that comes from being on the same hallway. She also required some teachers to rid their classrooms of extraneous materials that she thought made them feel like junkyards instead of classrooms. None of this won her popularity among those teachers already prone to not like her.

Among other things, some resented that Bolden had come from George Hall—which at this point was continually being held up throughout Mobile and Alabama as an example for what was possible. She arranged meals and celebrations for the teachers and—to demonstrate her fealty to her new school—she organized a food drive competition with George Hall to collect canned and boxed food. Gilliard being much larger than George Hall meant it had a built-in advantage, and it collected so much food it covered the gym floor—much more than George Hall had collected. "That brought us together because they hate George Hall," Bolden said, laughing.

The main resistance, though, was to Bolden's attempt to bring the kinds of systems that Bolden and Tomlinson had brought to George Hall: opening up classrooms and practices to scrutiny, collaborating, and establishing expectations for student behavior.

Even something as simple as making sure student work was displayed became a struggle. Displaying student work is a simple way to both motivate students to do their best and to allow colleagues to see what students are learning and doing. "I had to make it a directive," Bolden said.

MASTER SCHEDULES AND STUDYING DATA

That first year Bolden built a master schedule that meant grade-level teachers not only had fifty minutes a day of planning time but also common planning time, so that grade-level teachers could meet together and collaborate. Studying data to improve instruction was new to much of the staff at Gilliard. Bolden posted student reading and math data in a conference room used by grade-level teams and led discussions in grade-level meetings of what the data meant and how teachers could use it to think about what else they should try to help their students meet standards.

Even in her third year, Bolden said there was still so much grumbling about having to collaborate from some teachers that she had become annoyed. "They have more planning time than any other elementary school in Mobile," she said, saying she had arranged it that way so that teachers wouldn't feel that their lesson planning time was being intruded upon. "I have half a mind to go back to what they used to have."

But back to that first year: she and Turner took charge of discipline, regularly patrolling the halls watching for problems and handling them as they arose. Among other things, she wanted students to understand the expectations that they were to be orderly in the hallways and other public spaces and work hard in class. So, for example, if students were disorderly going to the lunchroom or physical education, they would spend a week eating or having P.E. in their classrooms. "It's about the expectations," Bolden said. Gradually, student behavior came into line, though it was still precarious because teachers weren't yet taking responsibility for student behavior.

She also spent that year building her leadership team, which included the assistant principal, the Title I facilitator, the counselor, and grade-level teachers, including fifth-grade teacher, Faith Lucy. Years later, Bolden said, "One thing about Faith is that in the classroom she was the best. She was always above everyone else. She was always a leader."

The leadership team focused on how to help teachers think about teaching and learning and acted as the communications hub of the school. "We were in the classrooms all the time," Bolden said.

She wanted the staff to have the benefit of her relationship with George Hall, and she and Tomlinson arranged for their combined staffs to have joint professional development focused on studying Common Core State Standards, which had recently been adopted by Alabama, developing formative assessments, and studying data.

"NEXT YEAR HAS TO BE THE YEAR WE TURN THE CORNER"

At the end of that first year, fourteen of the school's thirty-five classroom teachers and three of the six specials teachers left. That meant Bolden was able to hire teachers who shared her vision. During the 2010–2011 school year, her second, Bolden worked on incorporating new staff members into the team and putting more responsibility for discipline onto the teachers rather than treating it solely as a question for the principals.

For example, she and Turner worked with teachers to establish expectations and procedures for students who misbehaved—procedures such as time-outs, time in other rooms, and other methods. "Until they get used to it, it seems like extra," she said. Once the teachers and students knew the procedures, discipline problems dropped considerably.

At the end of the 2011–2012 school year, her third, she told me, "Next year has to be the year we turn the corner."

The following spring when I visited, she was less optimistic. "I was hoping to have this place in line in five years," she said, adding that she now thought it might take seven.

A few things had conspired against her during the 2012–2013 school year. For one, the district had forced her to take a teacher who had been let go by another school. "I had hired a great, great teacher—but [the district] wouldn't let me keep her because I had to take a mandatory transfer."

She was also still dealing with a group of teachers who resisted all her efforts, which, she said, was undermining the culture and climate of the school. "They ran the school" under the previous principal, she said. "It's hard for a lot of them to understand that we have to do what's best for our kids. Sometimes you have to make people see what the profession is about; it's not for a paycheck and getting off in the summer. And we have to work as a team."

The fact that the previous principal had not held teachers to account meant there was no documentation whether teachers were doing what they were supposed to do. That meant when Bolden documented their unwillingness to work collaboratively, "it looks personal." This made it difficult for her to fire or discipline teachers. She tried to transfer one teacher she was convinced could be a good teacher in another school, but the district told her that it didn't allow transfers—even though the district had forced a transfer on her that very year.

On the positive side, some grade levels had started working together wonderfully, she said. "They come to me and they say, 'Here's a problem and here's what we're going to do about it.'"

Another piece of good news: Swanee Terry became counselor. Bolden had inherited an excellent counselor, but she had left at the end of the previous year, leaving Bolden feeling bereft. Meanwhile, Terry, who had been a third-grade teacher at George Hall, had gotten her degree in counseling and Terri Tomlinson suggested that Bolden hire her. She considered Terry to be a great hire, and Terry quickly became part of the leadership team. Although Bolden was always conscious that Gilliard staff resented any comparison to George Hall, Terry was able to bring the ethos of George Hall that all students should be achieving in a nonthreatening way.

That year Bolden began requiring that teachers observe other classrooms. So that no one would think she was in some way being unfair, she wrote each teacher's name on a popsicle stick, and when a teacher was scheduled to do an observation, she had the teacher close her eyes, pull a stick, and then observe the teacher named on the stick. In one two-week period, there were eighty-nine observations. The teachers were unused to having their classroom practices scrutinized by other teachers, but "that has opened some of their eyes," Bolden said. Those teachers who didn't believe their students could learn to high levels saw students in some classes "actively engaged and working in groups." In others they saw students who weren't learning much.

"IT'S A NEW DAY"

A group of the most resistant teachers, mostly in the earlier grades, met every day after school to chew over their unhappiness. "If they spent that time working instead of complaining, they would be doing a lot better," Bolden said. Bolden finally brought the entire staff together to write the mission and vision of the school, but the simmering animosities kept them from making progress. "I let them say anything they wanted," she said later. "The big turnaround" was when one of the most successful teachers said to some of the other teachers, "'Some of us who are new think you resent us because we work hard.' You could have cut the air with a knife."

After that, Bolden told the group, "It's a new day. We are working together as a team."

Later she said, that meeting "was the one thing that changed the school."

All this time members of the leadership team were going to conferences and trainings, learning how to adapt instruction to the Common Core State Standards. They, in turn, led groups of teachers to study the standards and build lessons to help students read and analyze complex texts and understand and use mathematics to solve problems, two of the main aims of Common Core. Bolden and her leadership team were enthusiastic about Common Core, which they thought would help Alabama students compete nationally and internationally.

While the teachers were putting in all that work, the state school board was considering dropping Common Core because of a challenge by conservative groups. Coalitions of educators and business people—along with the governor—beat the challenge back, but from then on the standards were called Alabama State Standards.

At the end of 2013, Alabama administered the Alabama Reading and Math Test for the last time. Gilliard had showed considerable progress from when Bolden started, in math in particular. So, for example, 71 percent of Gilliard's third graders earned a level 4—the highest—on ARMT's math test. This meant Gilliard's students were performing comparably to Alabama's nonpoor students in Alabama, 71 percent of whom scored at level 4. Reading lagged a bit, but not much.

The next year Bolden moved some teachers around to different grade levels. Lynn Gullette, who was part of the leadership team, said that that shifting prompted some of the most resistant teachers to leave, but others began to see the power of collaborating and high expectations. "It can happen," she said, meaning that teachers can change when they are part of a system that supports good instruction.

Bolden began to feel as if Gilliard was really beginning to work. Teachers spent the summer studying the reading standards, mapping out curriculum, and realizing that the materials provided by the district were inadequate. They found materials or developed their own. Anything they wanted to buy, Bolden bought for them out of Title I funds.

All this time the teachers were working on the assumption that Alabama would administer an assessment tied to the standards, but here again state politics intruded. Alabama pulled out of both consortia that were developing assessments tied to Common Core Standards—Smarter Balanced and PARCC—and instead decided to administer the ACT Aspire. ACT Aspire is supposed to measure whether students are on track to do well on the ACT, a college admissions test, when they take it in tenth grade. Bolden said that with no established curriculum against which to measure themselves, elementary schools have to operate on what Ricardo Leblanc-Esparza, in another chapter, called "a hope and a prayer."

Bolden told teachers that they should concentrate on Alabama State Standards and let the assessment take care of itself.

Still, they scheduled some practice on computers with the tools and procedures that ACT Aspire would require. After the test was administered,

I talked with Bolden and once again heard frustration in her voice as she described how during the test a cut-and-paste tool that they had been promised would be available wasn't. "So it turned into a typing test," she said. Her students hadn't had a lot of practice typing on keyboards; for the most part they don't have computers at home, and the school had not focused on computer instruction during the school day. Students broke down and cried, she said.

When the results came back, Gilliard had performed respectably, not quite matching the state and district in reading, but outperforming both in math. So, for example, 54 percent of Gilliard's third graders earned either a 3 or 4 on the Aspire math assessment, compared to 52 percent in the state and 42 percent in Mobile.

That year when I visited, I talked again to fifth-grade teacher Faith Lucy, who said that before Bolden became principal, she had been embarrassed to tell people in Mobile that she taught at Gilliard. It had had such a terrible reputation that anyone who worked there was assumed to be a bad teacher. The old principal, she said, "loved the kids to death" but allowed teachers to do what they wanted: "everybody had their own rules." Bolden had brought "consistent expectations," professional development, and "a lot of training."

Teachers worked on helping students be more familiar with computers and help them better understand the kind of language and use of data that ACT Aspire uses. Test scores didn't improve much, but Gilliard was the only school in its area not to be labeled in need of improvement by the state's accountability system.

During the 2015–2016 school year—Bolden's seventh at Gilliard—she felt the school was on its way. Faith Lucy, who had finished an administrative program at the University of South Alabama, was now assistant principal. Although it was a bit tricky going from being a colleague to being a supervisor of the teachers, she said the process had gone fairly smoothly. Bolden said that although there were still some weak links, "Ninety percent of our teachers—if they went to almost any other school in Mobile—would be the best teacher on staff. And they want to be here." Students, she said, were getting "quality instruction" every day. Behavior was such that teachers were able to regularly take students on some of the same field trips that George Hall's teachers used to take, which was widening the their knowledge of the world. After-school and summer programs were well established, and the math team performed well against much wealthier schools.

It had taken years, but Gilliard had finally gotten a grant to bring mental health services to the school. Mobile Mental Health had begun staffing an office at Gilliard three days a week with counseling services both for students and families. In addition, a psychiatrist—able to prescribe medication—was at Gilliard one day a week. This emphasis on mental health services was a recognition of some of the serious issues students brought to school. For example, when I was there watching students arrive in the morning, I saw Bolden hand a student her walkie-talkie so she could search his backpack, give him a big hug, and send him on his way telling him to have a good day. She said she had to make sure he hadn't brought a weapon because he had threatened to kill his teacher. "He got here three weeks ago. He's starting to settle down." As another group of students passed by, she singled out one for a special greeting and a wish that he have a good day and said, later, that he had killed three dogs the previous week. One mark of the school's progress was that the University of South Alabama had once again begun sending student teachers to Gilliard. It had stopped years before because of the discipline issues. "It's taken all seven years to get to the point where they would send them," Bolden said.

MONKEY WRENCHES

A few monkey wrenches were thrown into what Bolden had hoped would be a smooth year, her final one at Gilliard. "If you had asked me before the beginning of the year how we would do this year, I would have said great. Now I'm not so sure."

At the school level, several teachers took maternity leaves and a few resigned, one because she wanted to stay home with a new baby and one because she said she couldn't support her family on a teacher's salary. Although Bolden said that she thought Gilliard was doing a good job supporting new teachers, it was hard to expect that students would do as well with new teachers as they would have with more experienced teachers.

At the school district level, the elementary school supervisors had issued directive after directive about changes to the district's curriculum, many of them being corrected multiple times after they had been issued. That had been confusing and proved to be a big distraction until the superintendent had stepped in and told the principals to do what made sense for their schools.

At the state level, the new teacher evaluation system that had been mandated required enormous amounts of time without, in Bolden's view, doing anything to help her provide professional development to teachers.

In addition to all of that, the improvements at Gilliard had meant that parents were no longer seeking to flee but seeking to enroll their children, which had driven enrollment up past 800. "They're using false addresses," Bolden said. The fluctuating student population meant that students who hadn't had the benefit of being at Gilliard were arriving all the time. "When you get students in the building who are behind, it is *hard*," Bolden said. "Our students come with no background knowledge."

Even more problematic than having new students arrive was that the state didn't give the school credit for those new students when it calculated staff allotments for the following year. Staff was allocated based on the average daily attendance for twenty days early in the previous school year. So new students who enrolled later in the year weren't counted, and because of that, Bolden would have to lay off teachers—"the teachers we want to keep"—over the summer. Even if the school was able to hire more teachers after school started because of the new students, the churn harmed staff cohesion and the collective knowledge that Bolden had spent years trying to build.

Another thing she was concerned about was how much emphasis the state was putting on assessment results, especially an assessment that seemed to her to be unmoored from standards and curriculum and that has no connection to student experience. "The first thing we tell students when we administer the ACT Aspire is that this test will have no bearing on your grades. They hear that this test has no affect on their future."

The pressures from the state to label schools as failing based on those assessment results, she said, makes it very difficult to lead a high-poverty school—particularly one with high mobility rates.

All of these uncertainties conspired to discourage Bolden.

PASSING THE BATON

At the end of the 2015–2016 school year, Bolden passed the baton to Faith Lucy, the teacher she had identified as a leader seven years before. "She's ready," Bolden said. "And let me tell you this. She is better than I am. There's not one other person in the district who could come in here and move this school."

She was assuming the district would appoint Lucy as her successor, in part because, she said, "There is no line of people who want to take over this school. This is a difficult school."

Even in the final days of Bolden's last year at Gilliard, she and Lucy had to meet with several teachers to keep them on track. "It's terrible, but you have to be relentless in your pursuit. If you let up at all, the culture can change back. It can start getting out of hand again." Some of the things they were concerned about: one teacher was out of her room "more than she should have been." Another was not checking to make sure her students were engaged and paying attention when she taught. Yet another showed a video during class. "We teach to the last day of school," Bolden said. "The very last day. We tell the teachers, 'You are not a babysitter, you're a teacher.'"

These issues point to something critically important, she said. "You can put things in place, but you have to monitor constantly. Little things can get you quickly off track."

Although Bolden technically could retire, she couldn't imagine not working. "I like seeing schools improve. I like seeing students learn," she said. "All kids have it in them. You just have to find what makes them tick. Every child has the right to be successful and to be able to learn."

In the summer of 2016 Lucy was indeed named principal of Gilliard and Bolden took a job in a middle school near where her parents live that has been low performing for years. I'm hoping I can watch her transform that school right from the beginning. She told me there's a pretty good hotel nearby that's not too expensive.

SYSTEMS TO NOTE

- A master schedule that provides common planning time for grade-level teachers.
- A system of discipline that focuses on helping students learn what is expected of them and builds relationships.
- A system of collaboration that focuses on standards, curriculum, and studying data to make plans for what else teachers can do.
- A system of getting students more time through after-school and summer programs and providing students and families with counseling and mental health services.

A FEW OBSERVATIONS

- Improving a school like Gilliard, which had been allowed to fall into a deplorable state, is really hard work. And it requires time—time to build the expertise and cohesion of the staff; time to build relationships with students, parents, and community members; time to develop the vocabulary and background knowledge of students. It took longer than George Hall took possibly because Bolden had much less leeway than Tomlinson had had in building a staff that shared her vision of student success.
- At the heart of what Bolden did was to organize the work of teaching and learning in ways that opened classrooms to scrutiny and thus improvement. This required reorganizing the way time was used to maximize time for instruction as well as teacher collaboration.
- Important to the improvement at Gilliard were counseling and mental health services, after-school programs, and other things that are sometimes referred to as "wrap-around" services.
- None of the work Bolden and the rest of her leadership team did would have been possible without a deep belief in the capacity of all students to learn and the belief that all students deserve a good education. The work is simply too difficult to undertake without that belief.

CHAPTER FIVE

Experts and Their
Systems at Work

Four Stories

The preceding chapter described the way Debbie Bolden took Gil-liard Elementary from a "hellhole" to a well-functioning school. In this chapter I describe a few other examples of expert educators helping dysfunctional schools become functional ones. By necessity, I am glossing over a lot of detail. By giving a few different examples, I am trying to un-derscore the kinds of systems experts put into place and the kinds of im-provement trajectories experienced by real schools. In the process I hope readers get a sense of how badly organized and managed some schools are. Finally, I want readers to see how expertise can be developed and passed along from one leader to a new generation of leaders.

JUNE ERESSY, CHANDLER ELEMENTARY COMMUNITY SCHOOL, WORCESTER, MASSACHUSETTS

I first met June Eressy when she was principal of University Park Campus School (UPCS) in Worcester, Massachusetts, which I wrote about in *It's Being Done*. UPCS is a small, high-poverty school serving grades 7 through 12 that was founded by Worcester Public Schools in conjunction with nearby Clark University. By the time I got there in 2005, UPCS was one of the top performing schools in the state, and two principals later it remains very high performing.

Soon after my first visit, Eressy agreed to take on a second school while staying as principal of UPCS. The school was Claremont Academy, a low performing Worcester public school that served students from seventh to twelfth grades who lived in the same neighborhood as UPCS. She served as principal for both schools for a couple of years and, she said, started making inroads on achievement at Claremont.

Eressy was making no extra money for leading two schools. With two kids in college and an ailing mother, she was drawn by the higher pay and lighter workload of a job in the district's central office. But she didn't enjoy it, and when her kids graduated, she decided, "I can't spend the rest of my career like this." In the summer of 2010, she jumped at the opportunity to be principal of Chandler Elementary Community School. Chandler had been named a "level 4" school by the state of Massachusetts, meaning that it was one of the lowest performing 5 percent of schools in the state. Under the No Child Left Behind Act, it required one of four "turnaround" strategies laid out by the federal government. The district chose to replace the principal and extend the school day as its intervention.

The school served about four hundred students from prekindergarten through sixth grade, most of whom were Hispanic and just about all of whom met the requirements for free and reduced-price meals. About 63 percent were English language learners.

When she took the job, Eressy told me, "I have three years to turn this school around," saying that her goal was to meet AYP in three years. AYP, or Adequate Yearly Progress, was an accountability measure of progress used by the federal government under No Child Left Behind.

When Eressy arrived, she found what she called a "toxic" environment. "It was like a battered women's shelter," she said, adding that the previous principal had blamed teachers for the school's low achievement and cowed and browbeat them. One example she gave was that a teacher asked if she could take a day off to attend her son's graduation. When Eressy replied that that was what personal days were for and she just needed to give notice, the teacher burst into grateful tears, saying that under the previous principal, teachers had not been allowed to take their personal days; she had missed her older son's graduation.

One teacher told me that the time she had spent with the previous principal was "six years of pure hell." The principal, she said, "would make fun of parents and would lambaste teachers in front of students." Another teacher told me that she had "nothing against him. He hired me, so I owe him." But, she added, she would see him only when things were going wrong and that he promised systems that never materialized. For example, when she first arrived at the school, she "heard about a mentor program" for new teachers but was never assigned a mentor. There hadn't been much collaboration among the teachers.

Unsurprisingly, Eressy saw her first task as building relationships with the teachers and staff. She met with each one individually to lay out her expectations and her vision that all students would show growth and master state standards.

As part of the turnaround strategy adopted by the district, teachers were expected to work longer days. A few teachers decided not to come back, but most stayed. Eressy's initial assessment was that although there were no teachers she would beg to stay if they announced a transfer: "I don't believe in just getting rid of teachers. You can help them get better." For her, the key was whether teachers cared for their students and had high expectations for them. If so, she could help them become better teachers. "I can't teach them how to love children, but I can teach them how to teach."

In general, Eressy said, the teachers at Chandler "loved the kids—to death. They had no expectations for them." She saw one of her jobs as helping teachers realize that the students could do more than they realized. She spent the summer working on the school's master schedule, setting up support for students and staff, and arranging for professional development for the teachers.

Knowing that she was eligible to retire in three years, she said, "When I leave, I want the systems in place so that the children get what they need." The kids had tremendous needs and few resources at home to support academics. She knew that if they were to master state standards, the school needed to be organized around instruction. For example, she arranged the schedule so that teachers had common planning times and then set up a schedule such that two days a week during their planning times teachers would meet by grade levels—one day to discuss English language arts and one day math. During those meetings they would go over the assessment data from the state testing, class assessments, and MAP testing.

MAP tests, developed by the Northwest Evaluation Association, are short computerized assessments that allow teachers to track student progress in both reading and math, and that correlated reasonably well with the state assessments. After examining the data, teachers would develop plans for how they would adjust their instruction. Eressy knew this kind of collaboration was unfamiliar to the teachers, so she or her math or reading coach were in all the meetings to help guide the discussions and keep them focused on instruction.

In addition to those collaboration meetings, teachers met one day a week during their planning times to talk about the school's culture and climate. And, finally, one day a week the collaboration time was dedicated to a meeting of grade-level leaders and the instructional leadership team to discuss instructional decisions that would then be vetted with grade-level teachers and, ultimately, with the faculty as a whole.

In addition, she set up two four-hour schoolwide meetings to discuss how teachers would have students write across the curriculum and two staff meetings a month for professional development. "Not housekeeping," she said firmly. She had heard that many of the staff meetings previously had been spent talking about things that teachers could have read about in e-mail.

For the professional development, she arranged for training in how to map out the curriculum in line with standards, setting up classrooms, and, from Jeff Howard's Efficacy Institute, developing high expectations for all students.[1]

When school started, she found that teachers were accustomed to developing their own curriculum with little regard for what students were learning at other grade levels. "Every level was teaching *Charlotte's Web*," she said. Since her background was in literacy, she taught the teachers how to assess students' reading levels, organize "guided reading" lessons in which teachers work with small groups on specific reading skills, conduct "read-alouds," and teach students to write in all the subjects.

She brought in Carenza Jackson, whose specialty was math, to be assistant principal, and Jackson worked with teachers on developing math lessons and modeled instruction so they could see for themselves what their students were capable of.

At the end of the year, Eressy said she was fairly confident that the school would see a bump in test scores because of all the systems she had put in place, which included after-school programs and Saturday school. And the school did see a bump. Not a huge one, but the student growth percentiles (SGP) leapt from 34 the previous year to 52 in English language arts and inched up from 49 to 52 in math. This meant that students' academic growth was greater than or equal to 52 percent of other similar students in the state. There was even a modest improvement in proficiency scores on the state test.[2] The state identified Chandler as a "rapid achievement gain" school and commended it for the fact that "teachers, instructional coaches, and community partners described the climate of the school as open and supportive; all of them credit the new leadership with this positive change."[3]

At the end of the 2010–2011 school year, Eressy was both happy with the improvement and impatient with the slow rate of that improvement. She said that she knew that teachers still didn't believe their students could achieve. "There's some remnant of the mindset that these kids will never be able to do it. The kids can do more than the teachers think they can."

Because Eressy was confident she was on the right track, the following year the school focused on incorporating the new Common Core math standards, which—among other things—meant teaching some things in more depth and reorganizing the order in which topics were taught. Jackson worked with teachers to study the standards, understand how to measure whether students had mastered the standards, and then develop lessons to teach the standards. She herself developed a lot of the materials, in part because she had little confidence in most commercially prepared materials and in part because many of the teachers didn't feel confident in teaching math and needed additional help and support.

Eressy led book studies among the staff. Doug Lemov's *Teach Like a Champion* and Paolo Freire's *Pedagogy of the Oppressed* were two of the books they studied.

At the end of the second year, 2011–2012, the scores dropped, most markedly in math. "I cried for three days after the scores came out," Eressy told me. "I was so upset because I truly believe—I know—they're teaching differently. I saw kids excited to take the test and tell me about it."

One possible explanation of the drop was that the school's embracing of Common Core math standards actually hurt it on the state assessment, which was still testing the old standards. That mismatch meant that students were tested on a few topics that hadn't yet been taught. The school's mobility might also have made a difference. "You turn around, and you don't have half the kids you started with in September." But Eressy was reluctant to cite either explanation for fear of turning it into an excuse.

She and Jackson focused on making sure teachers had clear information about which of their students were mastering the material and which needed additional help. To that end, they worked on helping teachers develop assessments that would be given at five-week intervals. "And we've been really strict about going back and seeing who's successful and who needs more help," Eressy said, adding that teachers were required to develop individual plans for students who were behind. In addition, Eressy and Jackson designed a number of interventions for students, including bringing in a part-time math tutor and a Saturday "boot camp" to do specific preparation for the state tests.

Routines of collaboration were still unsteady in many of the grade levels. "If I'm there, they collaborate," Jackson said. But teachers hadn't yet mastered collaboration enough to continue on their own. The key question Eressy and Jackson wanted teachers to focus on was, "At the end of the year, what do we need them to know, and what do they need to know for the next grade?" Teachers were still so used to simply marching through textbooks that they weren't accustomed to thinking in that way.

Eressy was also still seeing teachers using strategies she considered to be ineffective and that weren't supported by research. "They love to give homework," she said as one example. "And it's the stupidest homework—like spelling words five times. Name one person who learned from that." She thought reading should be the only thing that schools expect students to do at home and was not happy that teachers were still using whether students completed homework as part of grades. She found this practice particularly galling when students didn't have a quiet place to do homework. One student, for example, was living in a car with his mother and yet the teacher refused to take that into account in grading the homework.

Even with all of that, Eressy and Jackson went into the next round of testing reasonably confident. "I really believe we'll see a bump in scores this year," Eressy said. "If we don't, I'll retire." Jackson added: "And I'll be fired."

They did see a bump that year in 2012–2013. The growth scores in both English and math were at the fifty-eighth percentile, and proficiency on the state assessment was higher than the previous years. The school was no longer a level 4 school, in the bottom 5 percent; it was now a level 3. It was still in the lowest 20 percent of schools, but that was a huge step up. Even so, Eressy said, "We hadn't done enough to align the curriculum to standards."

They went into the next year with the wind behind their backs. They had added three new teachers because of increased enrollment, which gave Eressy a chance to hire teachers who shared her vision.

And they had brought teachers in for the summer to study the achievement data from the previous year and think through exactly what they needed students to know at the end of the year. From that, the teachers laid out clearly what big ideas they wanted students to master and how they would know if they had achieved it. They developed curriculum unit plans in which they thought through what vocabulary and other prerequisites were necessary and developed a plan for how they would build on prior knowledge and how they would handle misconceptions that would arise. They spent one week on math and one week on English language arts, working as grade levels.

"We had them start from the end goal and work backward," Eressy said. At the end of the two weeks, Eressy and Jackson had the teachers post their work on walls, and all the teachers studied the other grades' plans to ensure students would have a seamless experience going among the grade levels.

As the year unfolded, Eressy and Jackson realized that teachers were teaching the lessons but not assessing the students to see if they had learned the material. "We assumed they do the stuff we talk about. But they don't," Eressy said, adding that as a result the leadership team had intensified the monitoring they were doing. "When you see 80 percent of students not mastering stuff and the teacher has moved on," Jackson said, "that's a problem."

In collaboration meetings, Eressy and Jackson started having the teachers predict which students had mastered which skill. The leadership team then administered and graded assessments and provided the data to the teachers. Most teachers had wildly overestimated the mastery of their students. They were asked to analyze why they had thought the students had mastered more than they had and develop a plan for intervention. This was a difficult conversation for many teachers, some of whom cried. But, said Jackson, "We need to have honest conversations."

At the end of the 2013–2014 school year—Eressy's fourth—she predicted "steady growth," not a jump, and that's exactly what happened.

Eressy had stayed the three years she had planned on and one extra, and she felt Jackson was ready to become principal. She announced her retirement and hoped for the best. District officials, however, didn't appoint Jackson but rather a principal from another school. Eressy became a leadership coach working with principals and aspiring principals throughout the state, and Jackson is principal at another school in Worcester.

In 2015, because the school had met its growth goals, it was named a level 1 school.

Looking back, Eressy said, "Of all my school experiences, this was by far the most challenging and required the most malleability on my part." The most difficult element of the work? "Trying to convince faculty to adopt a growth mindset when dealing with students."[4]

FIGURE 5-1

Chandler Elementary School English Language Arts, Grade 6

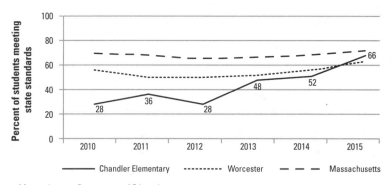

Source: Massachusetts Department of Education

SYSTEMS TO NOTE

- A master schedule that had uninterrupted times for instruction and common planning times for grade-level teachers to meet and instructional leadership teams to meet together.
- Systems for what would be discussed during the teacher collaboration times — standards, curriculum, assessments, and assessment results.
- Assessment systems to see which students needed additional help and intervention systems to help them.

A FEW OBSERVATIONS

- When Eressy arrived at Chandler, she found a school where teachers' abilities had not been respected by their principal, and that was mirrored in classrooms, where students' abilities had not been respected by their teachers.
- One of the lessons Eressy learned in the course of leading Chandler was that just because teachers agreed to do something in a collaboration meeting did not mean they would actually do it. She needed to ensure that everything that she thought important was monitored.
- Even with an infusion of a great deal of professional development focused on research and research-based practices, some teachers were still wedded to ineffective practices. This demonstrates how important it is for teachers to develop an evaluative sense so that they can dispassionately examine their own practices in light of research and experience.

RICCI HALL, CLAREMONT ACADEMY, WORCESTER, MASSACHUSETTS

Until 2012, Ricci Hall spent his entire career at University Park Campus School. As a student at neighboring Clark University, he did his student teaching at UPCS and then taught for many years before serving as assistant principal while mentored by June Eressy before succeeding her as principal in 2010. So he understood how schools were supposed to run and was accustomed to seeing students enter far behind in seventh grade, become good students, graduate, and go off to college.

As principal at UPCS, he saw his job as one in which he continually monitored and refined systems designed to make students successful. To give an example, while Hall was principal, UPCS began gathering data on how its students did after graduation. He and the faculty were unhappy to find out that although almost all students went to college, only about half actually graduated. "That's better than most high-poverty high schools," Hall said, "but our mission is to prepare our students for postsecondary education; that data meant we had to take a hard look at ourselves in the mirror."

To address the disappointing data, he led an effort to revamp the school's senior year to more closely resemble that of a college freshman, with syllabus-based classes that met only two or three times a week so that students would get used to the way college classes were structured. The faculty also developed a senior seminar to help students anticipate what they would encounter and to understand the organizational structure of colleges; they had realized that something as simple as not knowing that financial aid issues are handled by the bursar's office could derail students whose families were ill-equipped to advise them. The school developed a list of colleges where their students had been most successful and helped graduates develop a buddy system where upper-class UPCS graduates could help new freshmen. Those are just a few of the things UPCS did, but the upshot was that over the years, because UPCS teachers monitored and adjusted what they were doing, much higher percentages of students began graduating from postsecondary institutions.

All of this, Hall knew, was important, and he knew UPCS still had work to do to improve. But the fact was, he was a bit bored. Running UPCS was a matter of refining and renewing systems. He wanted a chance to put systems into place. In the summer of 2012, he got that opportunity at Claremont Academy.

"I Am Because We Are"

Less than a mile away from UPCS, Claremont Academy is also a middle-high school serving grades 7–12, and though double the size, it has pretty much the same demographic makeup as UPCS. About 90 percent of the five hundred-plus students qualify for free and reduced-price meals, and it has a large number of children of new immigrants, mostly from Central and South America but also from Southeastern Europe, Africa, and Asia. But instead of being one of the state's highest performing schools, it is a level 3 school, meaning in the bottom 20 percent of schools.

Much of the work Eressy had done years before had eroded by 2012. Pushing it into emergency territory was the fact that that spring only about 69 percent of students had graduated. In addition, suspensions were through the roof; college-going was low; teacher morale was terrible; and parents were complaining. The Worcester superintendent decided to take action, and appointed Hall principal and announced that all staff members would have to reapply for their jobs, which prompted protests and demonstrations by the teacher union. The district allowed Hall to bring with him a few key people from UPCS who were also looking for a new challenge.

All of this meant that Hall walked into a school that was unsuccessful, unhappy, and in turmoil. Many teachers were angry that they were being blamed for the school's lack of success, and they resented the highly successful and nationally recognized UPCS, which seemed to be invading.

When I talked with Hall that summer, he felt he needed to tackle three main things immediately: the adult culture, the student culture, and the foundational systems of the school—what he called "making the trains run on time."

Adult culture came first. He convinced district officials to rescind its decision that all staff members had to reapply for their jobs; instead, he asked staff members to "recommit" to the school. He talked with each of the forty-odd teachers individually, laying out his vision that all students would be good readers, good writers, and good problems solvers—that they be challenged to think deeply and be prepared for successful postsecondary work. He was initially buoyed by the fact that most teachers seemed committed to his vision and the school, but as the summer went on, many drifted away to other jobs. By the time school started, he had had to replace half the teachers.

The mad hiring scramble in August undermined one of his key goals— to get the trains running on time—because he couldn't build his master schedule until he had his full faculty roster. For example, he couldn't schedule a computer science class until he knew he would have a computer science teacher. His district supervisor started asking him not just for his master schedule but also for individual student schedules at the end of July, but every time he thought he was able to develop them, another resignation came in. That didn't reduce the district's demand, and Hall began to think his job was in jeopardy over the question. He had had as a goal making sure that every student and every teacher had a fully working schedule well before the first day of school, but it was clear that wouldn't happen. He finally told his supervisor that if the district wanted to replace him over the schedule, it could. It didn't.

Meanwhile, he faced other issues. Key was planning the week of summer professional development for teachers. He had identified that as an important opportunity to reset the adult culture and establish his expectations. He wanted teachers to have a logistically seamless experience to demonstrate that the school was under new, capable management, which meant he spent time on every detail of the week down to the pens and notebooks. But his main goal was to create "a community in which there was trust and collegiality." He wanted Claremont's faculty to collaborate in the same kind of deep way they did at UPCS, but he realized that would take time. "There wasn't enough trust to have the personal business of teaching being exposed," he said.

The last thing he wanted to do was use the words "At University Park, we. . . ." He knew that citing his experience at UPCS would raise the hackles of the non-UPCS teachers. He decided to do something new by drawing on a tradition of the regionally beloved Boston Celtics, whose coach Doc Rivers had used the concept of Ubuntu to draw together the team. Ubuntu is a philosophy common in southern Africa, popularized to the West by Nelson Mandela and Archbishop Desmond Tutu. Often summarized as "I am because we are," it draws on the idea that individual identity and worth are derived from the group. Ubuntu means that individuals support the group, and the group supports individuals. The Celtics attributed many a win to Ubuntu. "When things go wrong—and they will go wrong—we can use this one word to help us reset and recapture the mission," Hall told teachers.

Some of the professional development week focused on Ubuntu and team building, but most focused on instruction. He wanted teachers to think of themselves as providing "powerful learning experiences" for their students. Kate Shepherd, the math teacher he had brought from UPCS, did a model lesson in which she introduced a complex math problem and had the teachers wrestle with it to demonstrate the power of struggling to master a concept. One day of the professional development week was held at neighboring Clark University where professors who had worked with UPCS worked with Claremont's teachers. Hall thought this change of venue achieved three purposes: demonstrating his respect for the professionalism of the teachers by taking them off campus to a university; taking advantage of an important local resource; and, finally, demystifying for Claremont's teachers the relationship between Clark University and UPCS. Many Worcester teachers seemed to think UPCS had an enormous advantage in its relationship with Clark, and Hall wanted Claremont's teachers to know that whatever benefits UPCS had derived were also available to Claremont. For its part, the folks at Clark's Center for Urban Education were happy to establish a relationship with Claremont. Part of the reason they had cofounded UPCS back in 1996 had been that they had not been able to establish working relationships with existing Worcester schools, including Claremont.

Hall deliberately didn't focus on data. Bob Knittle, who had come with him from UPCS as instructional coach, had a large binder of data from the state assessments, including item analyses, collated by class and subject. So they had the data and knew the data well. But they both wanted teachers to think of data as answering questions and raising more questions. They didn't want teachers to feel overwhelmed and punished by the data. Also, Hall had been told that in the past Claremont had been way too focused on the state assessments, doing lots of test-prep. That's not what he wanted. He was convinced that if the teachers provided powerful learning experiences aimed at helping students master college-ready standards, test scores would take care of themselves.

The final day of that intense professional development week ended with a pot luck barbeque for all the teachers and their families. Hall was ebullient afterward. Staff members had shared treasured family recipes and broken bread together—a traditional way to build a sense of community—and the husbands of long-time teachers had told him that their wives were more excited about school opening than they had been in many years. The adoption of Ubuntu had been a big hit, and teachers were excitedly talking about "powerful learning," saying that they wanted students to "own" the classroom, have deep discussions, practice what they learned, and reflect on what they practiced. One said she was also excited that Hall and Knittle had said they would regularly observe lessons. "We've been so isolated," she said.

Hall still needed to make sure the trains ran on time, though. He and his team made sure teachers would have all the books and supplies they had asked for before the first day of school. As a nod to making a visible change in the physical environment, he arranged for people doing court-appointed community service to paint the hallways and entryway.

And then there were the lockers.

The student lockers were a kind that had five different possible combinations so that they could be changed from year to year. Set properly, all lockers would all be on the same combination, say combination #1. One key could then change an entire row of lockers to combination #2 and then the following year to combination #3 and so forth. However, homeroom teachers had been in charge of their classes' lockers and over the years had given different combination numbers to their lockers; the combinations were a mishmash and couldn't be easily reset. Hall decided to fix that issue so that in future years administrators would be able to easily change locker combinations. But that meant going in and adjusting each individual locker—a job that ended up taking about 80 hours. Hall himself spent some time on the project before he realized how time consuming it would be, after which he managed to hire some students who happened to drop by.

His focusing on the lockers reflected a deeper point. Hall sees the job of principals and other administrators as supporting teachers in improving their instruction. To him, one of the things that means is not offloading any more managerial and administrative functions onto teachers than absolutely necessary. Teachers should be focused on teaching and learning, not managing lockers. The lockers still needed managing, and for now that meant him.

Hall, Knittle, and Jim Looney, who had also come from UPCS as assistant principal, were finally able to begin working on the master schedule. When teachers began walking into his office to tell him when they wanted to teach which classes, he saw how the systems at Claremont had not been organized around student needs. He made it clear that the schedule would be built around the academic needs of students and the collaboration needs of teachers, but that didn't always sit well with teachers who had been used to a schedule built around when they wanted their planning periods.

The leadership team built a master schedule in which all students were in honors classes, instead of separating them into different academic strata. This was a major change, and to provide support to students who were behind, all the seventh- and eighth-grade students had "learning lab" during third period—when those students who needed extra help could get it. They also all had their elective classes during sixth and seventh periods so that grade-level teams of teachers could meet.

The ninth, tenth, and eleventh graders had their learning lab time during fourth period, and seniors had a senior seminar during which they would learn about the different postsecondary options, including job training, two-year and four-year colleges, and how to apply to college. But their teachers, too, had common planning periods by grade-level teams. In addition, on Fridays all teachers would meet with small cohorts of students in "advisories" with the idea that they would keep track of those students and how they were doing. The advisory teacher was the adult whom students could go to with any issues they were having.

With the master schedule done, they got to work on individual student schedules, but these schedules couldn't be completed. Students would have to choose their electives on the first day of school, after which they would receive their final schedules. The incomplete schedules were one more thing to keep the school from Hall's dream of a school that jumped right into instruction on the first day.

Just before school began, the teachers returned for a couple of professional days, and Hall tried to rekindle their enthusiasm for Ubuntu and powerful learning. But there were a lot of logistics to get through, including state-mandated trainings on bullying, the physical restraint of students, emergency evacuation procedures, ways to report suspected abuse and neglect, ways to report absences, and myriad other details, including locker assignments, how breakfast and lunch would be handled, and a welcome-back video from the superintendent.

Hall tried to make sure teachers heard, over and over, that he considered them professionals and trusted their professional judgment, but he would then have to give them information many had heard dozens of times before about blood-borne pathogens and tell them when they would be getting their box of latex gloves. Later he told me he knew that legislators and state and district education department officials wanted to ensure that students were safe, but he was frustrated that when they mandated how this kind of information was conveyed to teachers, their concern sometimes interfered with instruction.

Still, there was excitement in the air as school was about to begin.

Then the students returned.

Most had schedules on the first day, but not all, which meant lines in the cafeteria, and many new students showed up to register, which meant lines in the office. And some students' schedules were wrong. Hall had told teachers to just have students go through what the schedule said that first day, even if it was wrong. "So if he says 'I don't want sociology,' say 'Well, sorry, but go anyway,'" Hall had told teachers in their logistics briefing. The schedule snafus meant Hall and the other administrators had to play defense rather than set the example they had wanted to set of focusing on instruction the first day. He had wanted to visit classrooms, greet students, and watch lessons but instead was consumed with solving individual student issues.

He was also already facing a bit of a staff revolt. Hall's plan to address student culture focused on creating a community of trust. He had declared that the school building would be open to students before and after school so that they could play basketball or other games in the gym without direct adult supervision. In addition, he said that students would no longer need bathroom passes.

Many teachers thought both ideas were problematic. They had seen how hordes of students had wandered the halls in previous years and thought Hall was simply asking for trouble. Hall wanted students to develop a sense of responsibility about how they spent their time, not simply comply with rules. But the fact that teachers were not in agreement meant he and Looney were on the hook to make sure that trusting students didn't let the school get out of control.

After the first hectic day, Hall reflected, "I could have been back at an efficient, well-running school. It would have been easy." But, he added, "I'm an adrenaline junkie. As much as the stress can eat at you, I thrive on it. I was yearning for a place that needs me."

A Tough Year for Mr. Hall

Hall believed that students would welcome the newfound emphasis on reading, writing, and thinking deeply. In the past they had, he thought, not been treated as the serious thinkers they were capable of being and would feel liberated by the new Claremont. That's how he would have felt if he had been in their situation.

And maybe that was true for some of the students, but many—particularly the senior class—were pretty angry. Teachers they knew and trusted had left, and school felt unfamiliar. Some openly refused to read more than a paragraph at a time. Though he tried to remain upbeat, cheering students on, telling them they were smart and capable, their obduracy shocked Hall. By the end of the year, he was happy the senior class was leaving. Though he was loath to admit it, he thought he had arrived too late for them.

As much as he had hoped to be in classrooms during that first year, he had found that his attention was continually drawn away—either by meetings at the district office or by the thousand-and-one administrative details that come with running a school where students are more or less continually arriving and leaving. Plus, he found he was doing a lot of talking with students who were thrown out of class or wandered the halls when they shouldn't have been. Three years later I talked with a student, just before he graduated with honors, who had been one of those wanderers. "Mr. Hall talked to me a lot about what my goals were and whether what I was doing was helping me meet those goals," he said. "He took a lot of time with me. I know he thought I wasn't listening, but I was."

All in all, though, it was a tough year.

Still, there were a few signs of progress Hall could hold onto: teacher absences were down, and so were student absences. Suspensions were down. Hall wasn't particularly concerned about that year's stagnant test scores; it was too soon to see them rise, he thought. The following year would be better.

The next year—the 2013–2014 school year—the trains ran better. Most teachers stayed, schedules were done earlier and contained fewer errors, and teachers spent less time in their team meetings complaining about students and more time devising solutions.

Hall and Knittle wanted to start prying open classrooms so that instruction could improve. They made plans for what they called professional learning time in which teachers would develop "collaborative lesson plans." The idea was that if a teacher was planning to teach a particular topic, he or she might ask for help from teammates, who taught the same students, to help make the lesson powerful for their English language learners or their students with disabilities. "Everyone has a role in making that lesson successful," Hall said. For the full cycle of problem solving, team members would observe the lesson and examine whatever product students produced during it and then discuss whether the objectives had been met and, if not, what the next step should be. This process had been inspired by the practice of lesson study in Japan.[5] In addition, they organized departmental instructional rounds in which, for example, all the English teachers would observe English classes to begin developing shared practices and language.

These were the most direct incursions into the privacy of classrooms Hall had attempted, and they weren't universally embraced. "Some folks drank the Kool-Aid right away," Hall said. "But some folks were very reluctant."

One of the things he consciously tried to model was exposing his own failures and mistakes to the faculty. "I had to share my own vulnerabilities so that they would start feeling comfortable sharing theirs."

After a tentative semester, Knittle said, "Not everyone buys in, but you have to start somewhere." The idea, he said, was to get teachers to a point where they are "willing to admit they have a problem and to have people not blame but help." Knittle was bucking the traditional model of coaching, which was designed to help individual teachers improve instruction in their classrooms. But he and Hall saw that model as simply intensifying the isolation of teaching. They wanted to increase the capacity of all the teachers to help each other. And that was a harder sell. Only a couple of teachers volunteered to submit their problems of practice to a collaborative lesson study process that year.

When I visited classrooms, little instruction could be called "powerful learning experiences." Some teachers—notably those who had come from UPCS, but a few others as well—taught lessons that were well organized around key questions with good content and were able to guide discussions. But other teachers could barely hold onto their students' attention—which I could understand because the work they were asking students to do was dull, repetitive, and more appropriate for elementary school students than middle and high school students. A chemistry class in which students were coloring squares from the periodic table sticks in my mind as an example from that visit.

And students were still roaming the hallways. Hall began assigning teacher aides and even teachers to herd students back to class.

Hall continued to have difficulties making it into classrooms, and that year, when the test scores didn't go up, he was distressed. He didn't believe in spending a lot of time focused on preparing students for standardized tests; he had thought that by building a culture that encouraged teachers to teach and students to learn, test scores would follow naturally. Having two years in a row of stagnant scores undermined his theory.

He began to look haggard. He had wanted a challenge, but this sometimes seemed like an untamable monster. I began to worry whether he would quit, and I wasn't the only one. "I pray he doesn't leave," Knittle told me. "If we're not there six years, it's not going to work.'"

A year later Hall told me that I was right to have been worried. He had been tempted not just to quit but to leave education altogether. He is a paramedic, and he had started thinking about fully entering the health field. He didn't leave, though, and he didn't change course. He was convinced he was doing what was indicated by the best research and what he had seen work at University Park. He and Knittle redoubled efforts to build a culture of instruction among teachers, a culture of learning among students, and having the trains run on time.

But that fall, the beginning of the 2014–2015 school year, the festering unhappiness of a few teachers erupted. Their focus had to do with the fact that in Worcester, the teachers' contract says that high school teachers teach five out of seven periods and middle school teachers teach four out of six periods. As a combination middle-high school, Claremont had always scheduled its middle school teachers to teach five out of six periods.

This practice had gone on for many years before Hall, but technically 100 percent of the teachers had to agree. When some teachers filed a grievance, Claremont held a vote. All but three teachers agreed to teach five periods, but the three nay votes carried, and the master schedule had to be changed in mid-semester, causing huge disruptions and deepening divisions within the faculty.

At that point Hall came closest to quitting. But he decided that rather than quit he would lead the school in an application to the state for "innovation" status, which gives the school more leeway in terms of schedules, budgeting, personnel policies, and curriculum. Schoolwide discussions that linked back to the original vision of Ubuntu and powerful learning, Hall said, "created a shot in the arm for morale" and began to heal the divisions among the staff.

Meanwhile, the systems started to work better. The students who had been most inculcated in the culture of the old Claremont had left, and teachers started talking about instruction more and individual student issues less. More teachers participated in the collaborative lesson planning. A few of the school's highest flying students started taking classes at Clark University, and when they returned, they bore themselves a little differently and started exerting influence on other kids.

At the end of the year—finally—the improvements were reflected in a modest but real bump in the tenth-grade proficiency scores, which were what counted for graduation.

In the fall of 2015, Hall entered his fourth year confident Claremont was on the right track. And, he said, teachers had started to trust that he was not a fly-by-night principal about to leave. That year when I visited, I saw serious work being done in most classes. History and civics. Algebra. Discussions about literature. I don't want to exaggerate, but students were reading, writing, and discussing in academic ways. I didn't see what I had seen on previous visits—kids gossiping, goofing around, and annoying each other and the teachers. I saw a couple of students wandering but not the hordes of students I had seen before. Teachers said things like: "It was really rough there for a while, but things are definitely better now;" "Analysis may not be a word [students] are used to, but they're getting better;" and "The kids are doing more of the work and more of the thinking."

The school had revived its long-defunct membership in the National Honor Society and inducted eighteen students who had GPAs that made them eligible. "I'm hoping this will become a major force in moving the school," Hall said.

The faculty, Hall said, had begun to believe that "we're in this together and we're a team," which helped them "take the risk of opening their class to colleagues to solve problems." Hall had come in thinking it would take six years to get Claremont to the level of UPCS, and he had finally seen some progress. "That coherence, which is a hallmark of the work at UPCS, is happening here because of the structures to pry open the doors of classrooms," he said.

Hall was confident that the scores from his fourth year would show a bump. "I'm optimistic," he said. And when they were published in late September, they did show a bump. Eighty-five percent of tenth graders were proficient or advanced in English language arts compared to 90 percent in the state; 65 percent of them were proficient or advanced in math compared to 78 percent in the state. Claremont still hadn't met the goal set for it by the state, but it was getting closer.

FIGURE 5-2
Claremont Academy Graduation Rate, 2015

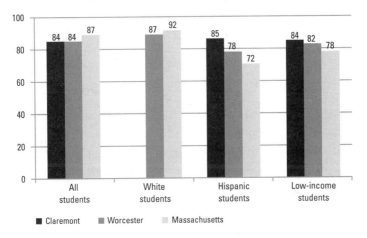

Note: Clarement Academy does not have enough white students to report separately.
Source: Massachusetts Department of Education

SYSTEMS TO NOTE

- A system of professional development that focused on providing "powerful learning experiences" and what they looked like and sounded like.
- A system of discipline that focused on developing a "culture of trust."
- A master schedule that put all students in the same level of instruction— "honors classes"—but provided extra time in "learning labs" that provided extra help and support to students who needed it.

A FEW OBSERVATIONS

- I've said it before, but it bears repeating: school improvement is not a quick process. Although some measures improved in Hall's first year, such as suspensions and attendance, it took a while for academic achievement to improve.
- Opening up the classroom to scrutiny and thus improvement is not always immediately welcomed by teachers, and it takes concerted effort to help them feel that outside observation is not an incursion on intimate private practice but rather a way to find help and support.
- Even a leader whose main focus is on improving instruction can find his attention diverted when there are too many logistical details to be attended to, and that may have slowed the school's academic progress.

KENNARD BRANCH, GARFIELD PREP, WASHINGTON, D.C.

The story of Kennard Branch and Garfield Prep actually begins in M. Hall Stanton Elementary School in North Philadelphia.

Stanton was a high-poverty school that I wrote about in *It's Being Done* when its principal was Barbara Adderley. This is how Barbara Adderley described the school that greeted her when she became principal in 2001:

> These were the most vulnerable children in the community and because there was no belief they could learn, the children had taken ownership of that. The principal was incompetent and the teachers closed

themselves in their rooms. . . . Attendance was not good. Parents were out of control. . . . The school was dirty; it was not child-centered; it certainly wasn't safe.

By the time I got to Stanton in 2005, the school was calm and pleasant and kids were learning everywhere I went, but the memory of what they called the "third- and fourth-grade gang wars" between students in the hallways was still very much in teachers' minds. Under Adderley's leadership, Stanton had gone from being one of the lowest performing—and most out-of-control—schools in Philadelphia to performing at levels above the average in Pennsylvania.

Then, in 2007, Adderley took a job as a regional superintendent in her hometown of the District of Columbia. She felt confident she was leaving the school in good shape; three people had the proper certifications to become principal, and they were all fully trained in the systems she had put into place. However, the district chose to put as principal someone from outside the school who quickly undid every system Adderley had established. The new principal dismantled the data collection and analysis systems; she tore down the data walls; and she canceled the grade-level collaboration meetings, staff retreats, and weekly professional development for new teachers. The school almost immediately began hemorrhaging staff, and achievement dropped like a rock. Within a year discipline was once again out of control, and a few years later the district closed the school.

As Stanton was falling apart, Adderley and I had many woeful conversations in which I could hear the disappointment and frustration in her voice. She had put her heart and soul into Stanton and had built the kinds of systems that could have sustained it in the hands of expert teachers and leaders, whom she had developed and left in place. Instead, it was destroyed, with dire consequences for the children of that neighborhood.

I consider Stanton to be one of the tragedies of American urban education.

Even so, Adderley's influence continues through the people she helped develop and train. One is Chrissy Taylor, who was a fifth-grade teacher when Adderley arrived at Stanton. For most of Adderley's tenure, Taylor served as math coach, and after Adderley's departure, she became principal of high-poverty Eisenhower Middle School in Norristown, Pennsylvania.

Another is Kennard Branch, who was a teacher at Stanton whom Adderley first developed as a school leader and then recruited as a principal in Washington, D.C. In the summer of 2012, Branch was appointed principal of Garfield Prep, which primarily serves African American students from low-income families. When he was appointed, Garfield was not only one of the lowest performing schools in the city, but it also had very serious discipline problems.

Over the next couple of years, under Branch's leadership, the school has become a calm, pleasant place where kids are learning. But there were lots of changes that had to happen to transform it. Here's just one that stands out to me. The school had almost no books when Branch arrived. Teachers would photocopy pages and staple them together to create little readers children could use. Branch was horrified and spent as much of his Title I money as he could on books and applied for additional grants so that he could fill classroom and school libraries.

Purchasing books was part of a larger focus on academics. "I really focused on instruction first," Branch told me. "I figured that better instruction would handle 80 percent of the behavioral problems." He developed common planning schedules so that teachers could collaborate, during which time they studied the data, studied student work, and planned adjustments in their instruction. In addition, he instituted three-week cycles in which teachers from each grade level would meet after school for two hours with him and his instructional leadership team to study standards, develop ways to assess whether students had met the standards, and draw up engaging, interesting lesson plans to teach the standards.

"That's what a master schedule with common collaboration periods affords you. If you grow together and learn together, it reduces the isolation of individual classrooms," he said. In addition, he and his leadership team regularly observed classrooms and provided teachers with feedback.

For the 2015–2016 school year, the district scheduled half an hour every morning during which all teachers in the district were supposed to collaborate. To Branch, such short blocks of time weren't useful, so he negotiated with his teachers that instead of meeting half-an-hour a day, the entire faculty would meet together after school for two hours a week to examine data and student work and work collaboratively to address instructional issues.

When I asked him whether he had initially welcomed collaboration when he was a teacher back at Stanton, he laughed and said no. "Ms. Adderley had to drag me out of my classroom," he told me. "Initially, all I wanted was to get back to my classroom and work on my lessons. I didn't see the point." Without Adderley's insistence, he said, he would still be in a classroom trying to be a great teacher all by himself. But, he added, he now realizes it is impossible to be a truly great teacher in isolation. Teachers can never know enough and be skillful enough to successfully teach all their students; teachers need the collective knowledge and skill of their colleagues and, sometimes, outside experts.

Since his arrival, students have soared in reading and math on the internal measures the school and district use. But when they took the new PARCC assessment in 2015, only a few students scored as proficient.

PARCC is widely thought to have set a much tougher bar than measuring grade-level standards, but that doesn't mean Branch thinks his kids can't do well on PARCC. "They're as smart as anyone else" is a phrase he uses often. But PARCC isn't making it easy for educators. The only information he received from the testing is an overall score. "All it is is a name and a number. Kennard Branch 750," he said. "It is almost useless data." He had hoped that the school would receive much more detailed information about where students were strong and where weak so that the school would know that teachers should, say, spend more time on number sense and less on measurement—or whatever the data might show. "We end up disaggregating the local assessments, but they don't help because they're not aligned to PARCC," he said. Even so, he was confident that the second year of testing the school would be more successful because instruction was more aligned to Common Core State Standards.

When the data arrived, the school had a modest improvement in English language arts: 35 percent of students were at level 3 or above on the PARCC assessment in English language arts, compared to 27 percent in 2015. Math dropped a tiny bit. The good news Branch could hold onto was that Garfield's growth in ELA was greater than the city's.

Although improved instruction helped make Garfield a much calmer place than it had been, it didn't handle 80 percent of the behavioral problems, Branch said. "It was more like 70 percent." In studying the achievement data, the team found that 30 percent of students were not on grade level. "When I looked at who they were, many of them were the students who were sent out of class or suspended from school for misbehavior. They're as smart as everyone else," Branch said. "We had to find a way to keep them in school and in class."

He and his instructional leadership team decided to treat behavior as "the fifth subject" and developed what Branch calls the "behavioral instructional leadership team" consisting of Branch, a school psychologist, two social workers, and a behavioral specialist. "It's really a mental health team," Branch said. They identified when students were most likely to get in trouble in which classrooms. For example, a teacher might tell them that during the second half of the literacy block or during transitions a particular student might start acting out. The team would visit during those times to watch for what might be triggering the incidents. Branch said that few kids would actually misbehave during those visits, but if they did, the team would do an "ABC analysis" of the antecedent, the behavior, and the consequence of the incident. "Sometimes teachers were a trigger by their responses to kids when kids were upset; sometimes they were just punishing and didn't assign appropriate consequences students could learn from." Even if no students acted out, the team would confer and then provide teachers with one or two things they could try. For example, they might suggest cutting down the time teachers fumbled with materials by preparing them ahead of time, because they could see students getting bored. To provide additional help, the district's specialist in autism education came to the school to help teachers think about how to manage classroom behavior.

Over time behavior problems dropped. First, there were forty students Branch called "high-flyers," then thirty, then ten. By the end of the 2015–2016 school year, they had three students who, "if they give you a good day, you thank God and move on," he said. All three, he said, had parents who refused medication and therapy for them as prescribed by doctors.

I include that story to demonstrate the way Branch thought, as coached by Adderley. When faced with an issue, he quantified it in a way he could monitor, sought to institute a system that might help, called on expert outsiders, provided individualized feedback to teachers, and continued to monitor the data and collaborate to see if what they were doing was helping or if further interventions were needed. Teachers around the country will confirm that they are often simply told to handle discipline better without being given the careful, individual help that this kind of system provided.

> ### SYSTEMS TO NOTE
>
> - Systems to monitor academic achievement and behavior.
> - Several systems for grade-level teams and cross-grade teams to study standards, data, and student work in order to plan and improve instruction.
> - A system to identify students with behavioral issues and a "behavioral instructional support team" to provide help to teachers.

A FEW OBSERVATIONS

- Garfield wasn't the first school I visited that, prior to leaders who knew what they were doing, had problems ensuring that teachers had the books and materials they needed. But for a Title I school to have had almost no books was really pretty shocking. It points to basic lack of management in some schools.
- Kennard Branch, who has put in several systems to require collaboration at Garfield, was not predisposed to want to collaborate when he was a teacher. He had wanted to be left alone to be a good teacher in his classroom; it took an expert school leader to teach him that isolation would never lead to excellence.
- It bears noting once again—a school that has been allowed to fall into the kind of low state that Garfield was does not turn on a dime. It takes time for teachers and students to gain the knowledge and expertise to achieve at high levels.
- The behavioral system Branch instituted wasn't one that Adderley had employed at Stanton. In fact, I have never seen this system in any other school. The point is not that every school should use the same exact systems. After all, different schools have different contexts and different resources available to them. The point is that expert educators continually examine the data and think, "What more can we do to make it better?"

CRAIG GFELLER, WEST GATE ELEMENTARY SCHOOL, PRINCE WILLIAM COUNTY, VIRGINIA

To tell the story of Craig Gfeller, I need to start with Graham Road Elementary School, a school that serves the children of new immigrants, most of them low-wage workers in the Washington suburb of Fairfax County, Virginia. In *HOW It's Being Done,* I described the work Molly Bensinger-Lacy did as principal to take Graham Road from one of the lowest performing schools in the district and state to one of the highest performing.

Bensinger-Lacy left Graham Road in January of 2010, five-and-a-half years after she arrived—after the school garnered a National Blue Ribbon and just before a congratulatory visit from President Barack Obama. She had hoped that her assistant principal, Aileen Flaherty, would be made principal so that the systems and expectations she had put in place would continue. Instead, the district put in place a principal from outside the school. When the new principal hired a kindergarten aide without consulting the kindergarten teachers or the leadership team, his action signaled to the staff that he would not lead the kind of collaboration they had become accustomed to.

All the team leaders—teachers who, according to Bensinger-Lacy, were fully inculcated in the culture of high expectations and who led collaboration at their grade levels—transferred to other schools at the end of the school year. The next year the school's percentage of students scoring advanced on the state assessments dropped dramatically. The school held on in terms of proficiency, a fact that Bensinger-Lacy attributed to the continuation of Flaherty, instructional coach Marie Parker, and Title I coach Kate O'Donnell, who doggedly kept some of the collaborative systems going. But then they, too, left, and after a couple of years of decline in test scores, the new principal also departed. Graham Road is now once again among the lowest performing schools in the state.

If Stanton is a tragedy of urban education, Graham Road is a tragedy of suburban education.

Even if Bensinger-Lacy's work did not continue at Graham Road, it lives on in the work of people she has helped train and coach, both at Graham Road and since then in her work as a consultant and principal coach.

One of those who credit her with helping him succeed is Craig Gfeller.

While Bensinger-Lacy was still principal at Graham Road, Gfeller was appointed principal of nearby Camelot Elementary, and the school district formally assigned her to be his principal mentor. Camelot was a mostly white, mostly wealthy school that had recently had an increase in children from new immigrant families and low-income families. Its change in demographics had ushered in a fall in achievement. Even though it was still a relatively high-wealth school—it didn't qualify for federal Title I funding—Camelot's achievement was way below Graham Road and other Title I schools in the district.

Gfeller paid a great deal of attention to Bensinger-Lacy's advice and adopted many of the systems she had used to improve Graham Road. For the 2010–2011 school year, he recruited Marie Parker from Graham Road as instructional coach and the school's improvements accelerated; Camelot became one of the higher performing schools in the district.

For the 2012–2013 school year, Gfeller was recruited away from Camelot, and the district appointed Aileen Flaherty, the former Graham Road assistant principal, as principal. Bensinger-Lacy called her appointment a "savvy one" because Flaherty had helped create many of the collaborative systems Gfeller and Parker had instituted. Camelot remains one of the higher performing schools in the district.

I include all those details to show how schools depend on the culture and systems that experts put in place—and how that expertise is developed and dispersed. And, finally, to note that putting the right principal in place—the responsibility of the school district—can make or break a school.

In any case, Bensinger-Lacy often told me of the work Gfeller was doing, first at Camelot and then at his new school—West Gate Elementary in Prince William County. Prince William County is an outer suburb of Washington, D.C., that not long ago was mostly farmland and today serves a diverse mixture of students. West Gate primarily serves the children of low-income immigrant families from Central and South America. Gfeller was recruited in part because no principal in the district had wanted to take the job. "I had a principal tell me he would never go to West Gate," Gfeller told me. "I told him, 'You're not lucky enough to have West Gate.'" I feel the need to say that Gfeller is very mild mannered. Meeting him, you wouldn't think he could say something so hard-edged.

When he arrived, West Gate was the lowest performing school in the county and one of the lowest performing schools in the state, but achievement wasn't the only thing wrong. Teacher turnover was high; teacher morale was worse; student behavior was terrible; and the building itself was filthy, which Gfeller called "a metaphor for the school."

When Gfeller arrived at West Gate, he shared his vision of helping all kids be successful with the staff. To accomplish that, he wanted to develop a "high-functioning professional learning community." He began with the master schedule, arranging it so that, in his words, "instruction drives the schedule; the schedule doesn't drive instruction." The old schedule, he said, had been fractured so that instructional blocks were interrupted by the specials—that is, art, music, physical education. He arranged it so that all students had uninterrupted blocks of instruction for reading, math, science, and social studies and so that all teachers on a grade level had the same planning time five days a week.

"To me, that's the easy part," he said about building the master schedule. "The hard part is what you do with that time. What are we doing with those instructional blocks and the planning time?"

To begin with, he said, teachers didn't know how to plan together. "They had planned field trips and things like that. There was no real instructional planning or collaboration."

Gfeller wanted the kind of professional learning community espoused by national consultants and authors Richard and Rebecca DuFour, whose work Bensinger-Lacy had used and adapted in her work at Graham Road. The DuFours urge schools to develop collaborative cultures, focused on results, that keep four questions in mind at all times:

- What do we want each student to learn?
- How will we know when each student has learned it?
- How will we respond when a student experiences difficulty in learning?
- What will we do if they already know it? [6]

Gfeller required that teachers collaborate three times a week with appropriate specialists. For example, the math coach would be there on the day they were talking about math, and the English language teacher would be present to help teachers think about how to adjust instruction for students still learning English. This requirement was critical, since about 60 percent of Westgate's students were English language learners. And he required that teachers use the protocols that had been developed and adapted by the teachers and leaders at Graham Road. Each purpose— unpacking a standard, studying data, and planning instruction—had a protocol for how teachers would participate. The idea was to ensure that every voice was heard and each perspective considered within an hour block of time. Some of the teachers objected, saying that the protocols seemed stilted and restrictive. He told them that if they could develop better protocols, he would be happy to consider them. "They never came back," he said.

To help guide the kind of collaboration he wanted to see, Gfeller and his assistant principal, Julie Svendsen, both sat in on the meetings, at least initially. Later they were able to split the responsibility, but Svendsen wasn't used to guiding instruction; her previous principal had mostly used her as a disciplinarian rather than an instructional leader. Gfeller wanted to model for her what he expected so that she would be prepared to be principal one day. In many ways this represented an extraordinary administrative effort; they were both in collaboration meetings for eighteen hours a week—three for every grade level from kindergarten through fifth grade. Gfeller reasoned that collaboration improved instruction; instruction improved the school. Therefore, the collaboration meetings were where his efforts were needed.

Gfeller sent a "guiding coalition" of teachers to a conference to learn directly from the DuFours, and they came back and brought what they had learned to the rest of the staff. He had dismantled the old leadership team because he had found that the hierarchy stifled rather than encouraged collaboration. So, for example, when he developed a vertical alignment team with the task of ensuring that the curriculum students experienced was aligned from grade to grade, he invited all teachers to be part of it. He needed at least one person to represent each grade level, but "three or four is fine," he said. Similarly, he gave all teachers opportunities to go to professional development at conferences or at district meetings, as long as they brought back what they learned to their colleagues.

It took a while for teachers to feel comfortable with the give and take of collaboration. "I like to debate because out of debate come better ideas,"

Gfeller said. One of his favorite questions is, "Why do we do things that way?" Initially, he said, teachers would shrink from that kind of discussion and become defensive. "It was almost a battered woman syndrome," he said. But over time teachers became more able to explain why they were doing what they were doing.

In the spring of 2015, he asked Bensinger-Lacy to sit in on some grade-level teacher collaboration meetings. She invited me to tag along, and I saw for myself the power of the systems he had instituted.

Teachers were confidently tackling the kinds of knotty teaching problems that Gfeller—and the DuFours—had envisioned. So, for example, we sat in on a fourth-grade math collaboration. The math coach told the teachers that the fifth-grade teachers were having to reteach fourth-grade material because students weren't able to put different fractions in size order. Being able to order fractions requires understanding that $\frac{3}{5}$ of an object is larger than $\frac{4}{10}$ and smaller than $\frac{13}{20}$, and that requires an understanding of what fractions represent. Clearly, the teachers had spent time in the past discussing how to teach fourth graders to understand fractions, but they went at the question with fresh energy. I didn't see any signs of defensiveness on the part of the teachers. No one questioned the judgment of the fifth-grade teachers. They simply went to work to do a better job than they had done the previous year.

Teachers agreed that by the end of the fraction unit students should be able to order six fractions, some of which would be improper, but that Friday they would all ask students to order the same four fractions—$\frac{3}{5}$, $\frac{11}{10}$, $\frac{2}{4}$, and $\frac{7}{8}$. That is to say, they agreed on what students needed to know and how and when they would assess it.

They then talked in detail about how they would help students understand fractions. It turned out that they had all been talking about fractions solely as fractions of a whole. But students weren't making the leap that $\frac{3}{4}$ of a chocolate bar represented a space on a number line. "They're thinking it's a chocolate bar," one teacher said. "They're not making the connections."[7]

They discussed introducing the topic to students by using grid paper, number lines, manipulatives, and models. They agreed they would have children work in small groups to find solutions and use exit tickets to "find kids we might want to look at," as one teacher said.

This teacher was thinking about identifying students who didn't understand the ordering of fractions after core classroom instruction and was referring to the fact that built into the schedule every day is twenty-five minutes for each grade level for "intervention"—that is, additional help for students who haven't quite grasped a concept during classroom instruction. Two days a week intervention was in class; three days a week students who needed intervention would go to a resource room. When I was there, Gfeller had started focusing on the fact that some interventions should be for students who already grasped concepts and could move on. "We have kids who need enrichment," he said.

For the most part, Gfeller and Svendsen participated in the fraction discussion that day by listening rather than talking, but Gfeller did offer that "I would give them some uncommon fractions" to really ensure that the students understood the concepts.

Each of the team discussions Bensinger-Lacy and I sat in on that day focused with the same level of detail guided by the same questions:

- What standards did students need to master?
- How would teachers know if they had mastered them?
- How would teachers teach it?
- What would they do if students didn't grasp it during core instruction?

I could see that this was how West Gate had made the progress it had. "The magic is not in the plans—it's in the process," Gfeller said.

That doesn't mean that instruction at West Gate was perfect. Gfeller said that there was still a lot of work to do to improve core instruction. Too many teachers, he said, relied on the interventions rather than focusing on improving the initial instruction the students received. But, he said, "We've reaped the low-hanging fruit—like teaching the curriculum." That was his way of saying that when he arrived, teachers really hadn't been teaching students what they would be asked on the annual state assessment, such as locating fractions on a number line.

The progress was reflected in one of the comments of a fourth-grade teacher during the collaboration meeting about "all the heartache the first year." When the teachers had first started looking at what the state assessment actually required students to do, she said, "I couldn't believe they had to do this. And now I think it's so easy!"

Gfeller had asked Bensinger-Lacy to sit in so that she could let him know what more could be done to improve the collaborative process. She had a few suggestions regarding the collaborative team meeting we saw that was focused on literacy: she thought the expectations of the teachers were not high enough in terms of what they were expecting students to read and discuss. For the most part, she said, Gfeller had learned what she had to teach and the collaboration meetings were achieving their purpose. She considered herself to have been an aggressive leader, but by requiring three collaboration meetings a week right from the beginning, Gfeller had been more aggressive than even she had been at Graham Road. And he had gotten even faster results.

"We didn't have the luxury of being gradual," Gfeller told me. "We were one of the lowest performing schools in the state." Besides, he said, "I knew that if I didn't move quickly, Molly would be upset with me."

One of the things Gfeller was proud of was that some grade levels had decided that collaboration was so powerful that the teachers had agreed to meet the other two days a week on their own.

I should note that during his years there, collaboration wasn't all Gfeller worked on. He also worked to build a school culture that celebrated students when they were good citizens. Suspensions dropped dramatically and disciplinary actions dropped from hundreds in his first year to about forty in the 2014–2015 school year, and "most of them are pretty minor."

And, I should add, the building was shiny clean. The first meeting Gfeller had had when he arrived in the district was with the county's head of maintenance, who showed him the monthly inspection reports indicating how bad the situation had been. The county head was threatening to take over the maintenance budget and functions if things didn't improve.

"I shared the data with the head of my building maintenance and asked him what we would do about this," Gfeller said. "I held him accountable for being a manager and taking responsibility for his troops. I was also clear on my expectations." Gfeller still sees the condition of the building—now spotless—as a metaphor for the school as a whole. "It was partly empowering [the head of maintenance] to lead," Gfeller said.

After three years of Gfeller's leadership, the school was named by Prince William County as a School of Excellence. Not long after I visited, Governor Terry McAuliffe showed up for a visit. "West Gate," he said, "is an excellent example of what can be done."

None of that meant that Gfeller's fellow principals were visiting to see what it was the school was doing. Some of them made it clear they thought he was gaming the system in some way, and West Gate's teachers were similarly ostracized at district meetings. "Nobody expects our kids to do it," Gfeller said.

Gfeller himself believes all students are capable of academic achievement, a belief he says comes from his own personal experience growing up in a poor farming family in upstate New York. "My family was on welfare at one point. There was alcohol abuse and physical abuse." He himself wasn't particularly successful in school, but what made a difference for him were "people who believed in me and in education." One teacher in particular helped him, as well as his high school employer, who helped him fill out college applications.

His experience made him believe that schools have a unique obligation. "The route for poor children out of poverty is us," he said.

For the 2015–2016 school year, the district asked Gfeller to become an associate superintendent so that he could help other schools make the

FIGURE 5-3
West Gate Elementary School Math, Grade 5

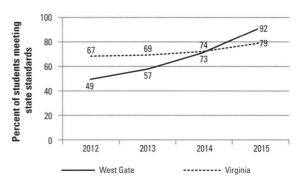

Source: Virginia Department of Education

same kinds of improvements West Gate had. Although somewhat reluctant, he agreed. Svendsen became principal, and the school, Gfeller told me, is doing just fine.

He is now working with a number of schools in Prince William County, trying to get them to adopt the same kinds of systems and processes he used at West Gate. "The principals who are seeing results," he said, "are the ones who are spending the time on collaboration."

He credits Bensinger-Lacy with helping him understand the kinds of things that could make a difference in a school. "I didn't start out this way. I became like this by listening to Molly and doing the things she told me to. She doesn't take credit for it, but her influence has helped many more kids than those at Graham Road."

SYSTEMS TO NOTE

- A master schedule that permits uninterrupted instruction in reading, math, science, and social studies and uninterrupted time for teachers to collaborate.
- A carefully developed set of procedures and protocols to unpack standards, map out curriculum, plan assessments, and study data.
- A system of monitoring that "empowers folks but also holds them accountable."
- A system of leadership development that allowed the school to continue the culture and systems after the departure of the principal.

A FEW OBSERVATIONS

- By making a proven principal an assistant superintendent, Prince William County is an example of a school district that is trying to ensure that expertise is learned from and dispersed widely. But the hostility and ostracism Gfeller and his teachers experienced from some of their fellow educators speaks to the difficulty many have in believing that children from low-income families can learn.
- As we've seen in other profiles, this one speaks to the power of a particularly knowledgeable and successful educator who is committed to helping other educators learn how to marshal the full power of

schools. In this case, Molly Bensinger-Lacy mentored Gfeller, who in turn mentored Svendsen. As I said in chapter 3, this process of replication might not be the fastest route to success imaginable, but it might be the most reliable.

- Unexpected school leaders come to their belief in students in different ways: Gfeller came to it through his own personal experience of poverty; Bensinger-Lacy came to it from her experience as a teacher, seeing her students learn. But they all have it baked deeply in their bones, giving their work what Gfeller and Bensinger-Lacy call a "moral purpose."

CHAPTER SIX

Why Expertise Is Not Enough

A Cautionary Tale

Tolstoy wrote: "All happy families are alike; each unhappy family is unhappy in its own way."

Over the years I have started to think the exact opposite about schools. That is to say, all low performing schools are alike; each high performing school is happy in its own way.

In a low performing school, where only a handful of students are proficient on state standards, odds are very good that discipline issues dominate adult conversations and administrative time; students and teachers have high absentee rates; and teacher and principal turnover is a significant problem. Teachers can say what their own classes are working on but have little idea what other classes are doing, and they often don't even know the names of teachers outside their grade or department. When you walk through the halls, you see students wandering; when you peer into classrooms, you see many teachers gathering or distributing materials, showing movies, trying to bring students to order, or sitting at their desks while students are doing very little. Not much student work is displayed, and what there is tends to all have been posted at the same time, as if to impress a visitor. Sometimes principals are visible but overwhelmed by crises; sometimes they are hardly to be seen. In any case, their attention is rarely on improving instruction.

Even the lowest performing schools will have one—or even several—orderly and focused classrooms where students are behaving and learning a great deal; the other teachers often resent the teachers in those rooms for having been favored with "better kids." To stay away from that kind of vitriol, the exceptional teachers close their doors, stay out of the teachers' lounge, and talk only to kindred spirits. That leaves the teachers' lounges as hotbeds of complaints and grievances.

I may not have described every low performing school in the preceding paragraphs, but I suspect I came pretty close.[1]

One person with whom I have discussed my all-low-performing-schools-are-alike theory is Ricardo LeBlanc-Esparza. Actually, he may be the originator of the theory; we've been talking about it for so long, I'm no longer sure.

Esparza's experiences provide a fascinating window onto American education, highlighting the fact that even when a school leader has a clear idea about how to help schools improve—and a track record of success—that alone isn't enough.

"IT'S ALL ABOUT THE SYSTEMS"

I first wrote about Esparza in *It's Being Done* (2007) when he was principal of Granger High School in the Yakima Valley of Washington. He had become principal in 2001 when the school had a graduation rate of somewhere under 50 percent of students (Washington state doesn't publish the records back that far). By 2005, when I visited, the graduation rate was about 70 percent. At the same time, the school's reading and writing performance on state assessments had improved markedly. That improvement—in a school where most of the students were the children of low-income farm workers—was significant; he made it look like a simple matter of common sense.

"It's all about the systems," he has said to me maybe a hundred times.

Since he left Granger in 2008, Esparza has been principal of three other schools and visited and worked as a consultant in a number of low performing schools in several states. Just by looking at the data, he could predict that a low performing school would have no systems to ensure that teachers and students knew how they were doing or to ensure that they were collaborating on how to improve. He also could predict that the systems in place to manage student behavior would be more about punishing students than building relationships and motivating them.

At Granger, Esparza had kept the emphasis on teaching and learning and built system after system with the purpose of providing clear information to students, parents, and teachers. It was the beginning of the era of collecting and reporting achievement and other data under federal law, so having that kind of information was still new. He was able to provide teachers with information about their students' reading levels and how their classes had performed on the state reading, writing, and math assessments the previous year. He asked teachers to develop a sense of where their students were, where they needed to go, and which aspects of their instruction needed to change in order to get them there. He also shared the school's data with students, many of whom, he said, were surprised that they were as low performing as they were. Because they had passed their classes in elementary and middle school, students had had no sense of alarm about the fact that they were not, for the most part, reading at a high school level.

A formative experience for Esparza came soon after his arrival at Granger when a mother asked about plans for graduation. He looked up her son's record and told her, as gently as he could, that her son was not on track to graduate. She was stunned and angry; she had sent her son off to high school every day for almost four years and had no idea that he had accumulated only a few credits toward graduation.

Esparza vowed that he would never let a parent be blindsided in that way again, so he set to work developing a coherent information system for parents. Up until then the school had relied on "back-to-school" nights when parents lined up to talk for a few minutes with teachers, who were stationed at tables ringing the gym. Only about 10 percent of the students' families had attended—fairly standard for a low performing school. Instead of continuing such an unsuccessful system, Esparza scrapped it. He began a system of advisory classes wherein twenty students were assigned to every professional in the building, including not just the teachers but also the librarian, the counselors, and himself—and scheduled them to meet four days a week, during which they followed an online guidance curriculum developed by the state. Esparza was mindful that the advisory classes shouldn't mean teachers had another set of lessons to prepare for, but he also didn't want the time to be wasted as it is in many schools. The state curriculum covered a great deal of ground that many teachers think students should learn about—how to balance a checking account, how to apply to college, how to apply for financial aid, and so forth—but there was also time for team building and helping students get and stay organized for their classes.

The core purpose of the advisory was to ensure that all students had an adult in the building who knew them well. "I can't ask teachers to coach 125 students," he said, referring to a typical student load of high school teachers. "But I can ask them to coach 20 students."

Then he required the advisory teachers to meet with every student's family twice a year, during which students led the conversation. Students followed a set protocol in which they would report to their families their career goal, what their reading level was, how many credits toward graduation they had earned, and how many more they needed and in what classes. The advisory teacher, armed with information from the student's other teachers, would add any necessary details about how the student was doing in his or her classes and what help the school was offering. So, for example, if the student was behind in math, the teacher would inform the student and parents of what help was available in before- and after-school tutoring programs.

At the end of the conference, the parents or guardians were asked to sign a contract as to what they committed to do. Usually, they were asked to get the student to school on time and either provide a quiet place to study or encourage the student to stay after school to work. The student would pledge to attend whatever before- or after-school classes the school advised, and the teacher would agree to provide all necessary communication in regard to student progress and behavior issues such as attendance.

This system was in many ways simple, but it ensured that parents understood how school worked and how their children were progressing toward graduation and that no parent would again be surprised as the angry mother was. This type of system was especially important in a school where many of the parents hadn't themselves graduated from or, in many cases, even attended high school. "My parents didn't understand the system," Esparza said, "but they learned what [the grades] A, B, C, D, and

E meant, and they knew how to monitor. That's the information parents needed which was provided on a bimonthly basis."

The advisory system also meant that there was an adult in the school who kept track of every student and could act as a liaison between the school and the family—and between the student and other teachers, who might need to know about family crises or other issues.

Finally, that piece of paper with the three signatures served as the way Esparza could monitor participation and hold everyone involved accountable.

Although some teachers welcomed the new advisory system as an opportunity to get to know a small group of students better, not all were happy with the idea and objected that they shouldn't be expected to be social workers. Esparza would point out all the good things that could come from this system, in addition to relieving teachers of having to sit through those back-to-school nights—which hadn't been satisfying for anyone. But ultimately if he had to, he would say: "You're a good teacher, but we have a different philosophy. I'd be happy to write you a recommendation."

In the first year parent participation was 30 percent, which the teachers pointed to as a great triumph, since it was three times the normal attendance at parent nights. "I said, okay, we can celebrate," Esparza said, "but we need 100 percent." Because he himself had an advisory group, he knew what the obstacles were: he had to call some families multiple times and even visit students' homes, some of which were tents pitched next to pickup trucks in the local mobile home park. One issue was that many students did not live with their parents, so grandparents, foster parents, aunts, and uncles needed to be enlisted. Esparza even met with a student's husband once, asking him to sign the contract that he would support his young bride's schooling. But soon the twice-yearly conference became part of the culture at Granger. For the rest of his tenure, attendance at family conferences was 100 percent.

As in many schools, teachers were concerned about student absences and made the argument that they couldn't be expected to teach students who weren't there. So Esparza set up a system that required students to make up any unexcused absences in before- or after-school classes to receive credit for a class and to retain the ability to play on a team or participate in a club. "If you miss an hour, you owe me an hour," he said, showing me the poster in the hallway with the names of students and the hours they owed. Attendance improved dramatically.

By the time I got to Granger, in 2005, Esparza and the faculty were fine-tuning these kinds of processes and beginning to put into place new ones. For example, they saw some real promise in professional learning communities being promoted by a number of professional organizations. Professional learning communities—or PLCs—are ways for teachers to work together to investigate and act upon data and evidence of achievement, and Esparza thought that structure might be helpful in driving professional conversations among teachers.

In the beginning, he told me, he had had to start with basic safety. In 2001 the town had the highest crime rate in the Yakima Valley, and not too long before he took the job, a student had been stabbed during an after-school fight and died in the gymnasium. Most of that first year, gang graffiti would appear on a school outbuilding every morning; he would spray paint it back to white on his way to work so that gangs could not advertise they were in control of the school.

Esparza banned the wearing of red and blue if being used as gang affiliation and confiscated all belts and bandanas that were being used to represent gangs. Esparza decided to tie confiscated bandanas together to demonstrate unity across gang membership. By the end of his first year, he had more than thirty bandanas tied together and was able to get the gang issues under control.

It would have been easy for him to see students acting out as bad kids who needed to be suspended and expelled. Instead, he saw "academic refugees," most of whom arrived in high school reading below a fifth-grade reading level. "How often have they been told, 'You are as dumb as a box of rocks'?" Esparza asked. Almost always, he said, students who were discipline problems couldn't read well. To solve the discipline problem, he needed to solve the reading problem.

He hired a long-time teacher, William Roulston, who, together with another teacher in the Yakima Valley, had developed a program that worked on reading fluency.[2] They had found that most high school students could decode but couldn't read quickly enough that they could remember the beginning of the sentence by the time they got to the end of the sentence. Esparza scheduled all students who read at or below the fifth-grade level—and that was most students—into a reading class using that program. The program built fluency by having the class read and re-read increasingly complex passages posing ethical dilemmas appropriate to high school students. They would debate and discuss the passage, with the teacher helping them learn the vocabulary and background knowledge necessary to the passage. In this way the students' intellects were being both respected and developed, and bit by measurable bit, their reading levels improved and students were reading longer works. The school also instituted Accelerated Reader, a reading monitoring system more often found in elementary schools, to monitor the independent reading prac-tice students were doing, and filled the library with easy-to-read, high-interest books.

Esparza was a continual coach for students, encouraging them to de-velop dreams and aspirations and then work hard to achieve them. He got a license plate that said "Si´ Se Puede," the slogan popularized by Cesar Chavez and the United Farm Workers that meant, "It *is* possible" or "Yes, we can."

"THREE! I HAVE THREE GRANDCHILDREN GRADUATING"

Knowing that 2008 would be Esparza's final year at Granger, I went out to attend graduation. This was the first class that had had to pass the state reading and writing test to be able to graduate, and throughout Washing-ton were dire warnings about students from low-income families not be-ing able to graduate as a result. Many of the superintendents in the Yakima Valley (including Granger's) had signed an open letter saying that their students shouldn't be expected to meet the standards.

That year almost 90 percent of Granger's class of 2008 walked the graduation stage—well, the gym floor—to the cheers of family members, and a few more students would graduate during the summer. Thirty-seven percent of the graduates were heading for four-year college; 40 percent to two-year college; and 13 percent to technical school, which meant 90 per-cent of the graduates were heading to some kind of postsecondary educa-tion. Considering that 79 percent of the graduates did not have parents who had graduated from high school, this was an emotional moment for many of the families.

"Most of us are Latino, so our parents work in the fields," said Miguel Garcia, a graduating senior who himself had spent many weekends and school vacations working in the fields. "We don't want to work in the fields our whole lives," he said, "so we strive to get out." He was heading off to Central Washington University, where he was planning on studying construction management.

A particularly moving moment for me was when a grandmother came up to me and held up a calloused hand with three fingers upraised. "Three!" she said. When I looked puzzled, she told me, "I have three grandchildren graduating today!" She told me that she had grown up in Granger and had wanted to get an education, but after her father died, she had had to leave school at the age of eleven to pick apples, cherries, and hops. "When my father died, all my dreams were gone," she said. Only two of her children had graduated, but she was hoping all sixteen of her grandchildren would graduate and go to college.

To me, her grandchildren and Miguel embodied the importance of the work Esparza and the faculty at Granger had done. "People have to understand that students of poverty can be just as successful as anyone else," Esparza said. "But it begins with the belief system."

Esparza had himself experienced the low expectations that schools had for him as a migrant student. Until he was in third grade, his family had followed the crops; in fact, he has a photograph of himself as a seven-year-old cutting asparagus. He vividly remembers his sense of dread walking into yet another new school and the relief he felt if he saw one of his many cousins there. Eventually, his parents saved enough money to buy a little land and stay put, and he found success as a high school wrestler, which gained him entrée to college and thus a career in education, beginning as a teacher and wrestling coach. "I come from poverty," he said. "I come from where my students come from, and I know if I can make it, they can make it."

Looking back on his experience at Granger, I could easily see that Esparza was drawing heavily on his coaching background, which had taught him that people—students, teachers, and parents—learn more when they have developed relationships of respect, have clear information about how they're doing, and have multiple opportunities to practice. Schools, he said, needed clear systems to ensure all those things, and he experimented with a number of different such systems. Most of the time at Granger, Esparza was pretty much "flying by the seat of my pants," he told me, because "there was no road map to show me how to go."

When he walked into his next schools, he was better prepared.

I was able to visit two of those schools, both of which demonstrated the power of the basic principles he had brought to Granger. But they are also cautionary tales, showing how incoherent some "reform" efforts are and how difficult school district politics can be.

One of the reasons Esparza left Granger was that on an educational trip to China, he had met a fellow like-minded educator who lived in Denver. He fell in love with her, and after his daughter graduated from Granger in 2008, he and his newfound love married and he moved to Denver. He found a job in a small district outside the city where just about all the students were Hispanic and 90 percent qualified for free and reduced-price meals.

STEPPING INTO CHAOS

Having led a great deal of progress in a difficult, high-poverty high school, Esparza was confident that he could easily handle an elementary school. That was before he walked in the door.

The school had been deemed a "turnaround school" by the state, which meant that it was one of the lowest performing 5 percent of schools in Colorado. The district had opted for one of the more drastic options under federal law, which was to replace both the principal and 50 percent of the staff. By the time Esparza was hired, the rest of the staff had been replaced, which meant he had lost a major opportunity to shape the culture of the school by hiring people who shared his vision. In addition, as part of its turnaround plan, the district had hired a "turnaround specialist," which meant that right from the beginning there was an unclear line of authority within the school. This confusion played out in a number of ways, including decisions not only about personnel but also scheduling and curriculum.

Esparza's first concern, however, was to address the school's out-of-control student behavior, which had resulted in through-the-roof suspension and expulsion rates the previous year. On his first day he saw one of the many problems. The school had a morning procedure whereby students would line up outside their classrooms and wait for teachers to open their doors at the start of the school day. When Esparza walked through the lightly supervised hallways, he saw bored students bumping and shoving, which quickly led to hitting and backpack throwing. "I saw I was going to have to suspend students before school even started on my first day," he told me.

He took immediate action, bringing all the students into the gym and calling all the teachers there as well. This initial gym meeting developed into a daily system in which the students and faculty would start every day together. Esparza reasoned that if you could motivate high school students with pep rallies, why not elementary school students when they are the most impressionable? The ten-minute meetings set the tone for the day and were opportunities to give a short motivational talk and recognize students for academic achievement. The whole school of 300-plus students said the pledge of allegiance, sang the national anthem, and heard any school announcements. And Esparza would give some version of his classic talk, "A dream does not come true if you do not work for it," complete with call and response: "Do you believe?" "Yes!" "Do you believe?" "YES!!!!!"

He spent a good deal of time managing behavior for the first few months, but he found that the morning assemblies were part of helping students "develop a sense of self as a member of a team working toward common goals."

Teachers affirmed that students had developed a different attitude. "A lot of kids were challenging the system in past years," said a fourth-grade teacher. "I'm not sure how he managed it, because he wasn't exactly strict, but [Esparza] would come down and have a talk and ask them, 'Why are you acting out?' He would have them read *The Little Engine That Could* and say, 'That's a kid's book, you should be able to read it easily. You have to step it up.'" And, she said, they would.

Another teacher gave an example of a particularly troublesome student: "He would say [to me], 'You're not my mom' and do anything to defy me. [Esparza] took him into his office and talked to him and I started to work with him and I changed my attitude toward him and he changed his attitude—and look at [how successful he is]. Now, every day I come to school, I come because of Carlos."

Esparza had the same basic approach to discipline that he had at Granger, which was to use misbehavior as an opportunity to connect to students' aspirations and direct them back to working on their academics. "I'd have students write what they want to do and post it up on the wall," he said. Then "if they're misbehaving or not doing anything, I'd point and say, 'Christina, I thought you said you wanted to be a nurse. Is that you up there? Yes? Are you going to get there by what you're doing now? No? Then let's get back to work.'"

Still, he was surprised by the level of discipline in the school. "I wasn't prepared for the chaos in student behavior," he said. "I got kicked, spit at. We had kids who flat-out thought they could rule the school." He ended up suspending fifteen students, some multiple times. Each time he'd bring in the parents and talk about the students' academic achievement. "I'd say, 'It's about your future.'"

Teachers were unused to looking at the state's standards or data, so Esparza spent time helping them look at the school's performance data through the framework of, "Look, here's where you are; here's where you need to be. Now, how are we going to get there?"

When I talked with teachers, many told me that for the first time they felt as if they were part of a team rather than working on their own. They studied the state standards that students were expected to master and developed plans to help them do so.

Esparza was adamant that schools need to hold students, particularly students from low-income families, to high expectations and be very clear and focused about teaching them a great deal about the world. "I have found that children who grow up in poverty, their world is pretty much limited to their little neighborhood and to their aunts and uncles and family barbeques and that's it," he said. "So when you talk about being a doctor or a lawyer or anything else, it's like saying 'Louisiana.' They've never taken geography or history, so they don't know our country and what states exist. They don't really have anything to ground and grab hold of. . . . How do we get them to see what's out there?"

With 80 percent of students reading below grade level, Esparza began telling students and their parents that they needed to read for an hour a day outside of school. "How do you work on comprehension skills?" he asked. "It's called program read-a-lot," a phrase he used to mock expensive and complex programs that weren't as effective as simple, dedicated practice. Students who live in poverty, he said, didn't get to travel the way wealthier students can. "With books, you can travel to another world, another reality."

In the middle of the year, he made some changes to the master schedule. For example, he ended departmentalization—the system whereby different elementary school teachers teach different subjects. "We lost so much time in transition," he said. "And there was no chance to build relationships. Once you've established relationships, then you can specialize." He also built into the daily schedule "flex time," which was time when students who were behind in reading or math would get targeted help.

One student who had recently arrived from another school was a testament to this system. "At first I didn't get multiplication," she said. "But they took me to the back of the room and worked with me during flex time," adding that she really liked the school and had started reading an hour a day at home.

Esparza found that many of the levers of change usually available to a principal had been assigned to the turnaround specialist, which limited what he was able to do. So, for example, as part of the reform effort, the district had partnered with an outside agency to provide after-school programming for students, during which time teachers were supposed to receive professional development. Esparza was not impressed by the after-school programming, which was taught by outside teachers and noncertified staff and put together very quickly without much vetting. He would have preferred to have classes taught by his teachers, who at least would be able to build relationships and school cohesion and at best would help students learn.

On my visit I was able to talk with the superintendent, and I could see what Esparza meant. The superintendent explained to me that he had decided to cut science out of daily instruction in favor of an after-school science class taught by, for the most part, a hastily assembled group of college students. I asked him what the curriculum of the after-school class was, and he said, "Funny story!" He proceeded to tell me about running into a friend who knew someone from a publishing company that, needing to pilot its new science curriculum, provided it to the district for free.

The students in that school needed the best possible curriculum, one that was aligned to the state's science standards and had been tested and found to be sound and effective. Instead, the superintendent was allowing his very vulnerable students to be taught an unproven curriculum by people who weren't even teachers because of a chance encounter with a friend. This is a prime example of how some people in education make decisions that lead to incoherence and low performance.

Predictably, the school that had achieved calm during the regular school day became chaotic and out-of-control after school.

Frustrated that he had no control over what happened after school, Esparza kept trying to work on the things he did have control over. So, for example, he instituted student-led parent–teacher conferences, similar to those at Granger. However, because the turnaround specialist had control of teachers' professional development and much of the state grant budget, Esparza's ability to make improvements in instruction was compromised. Even so, many of the teachers who had been at the school since before the turnaround recognized that Esparza was fighting for the kinds of things that would make it a better school to teach in. One mark of that was that the school's union shop steward, who had lived through multiple principals in the previous ten years, met regularly with him to try to help him navigate the tricky district politics.

"This is the hardest thing I've ever done," Esparza told me about feeling responsible for the results of the school without having the appropriate level of authority. Frustrated, Esparza reluctantly left this position at the end of the year.

To me, Esparza's experience was a clear example of a well-intentioned and badly managed reform. The state had provided the district with a three-year multimillion dollar grant to turn the school around as part of a federal turnaround effort. But with lots of plans and programs and very little coherence, the district's efforts didn't build the systems that would lead to improvement and undermined Esparza, thus making the money fairly useless.

Even with all the problems, in the year Esparza was there, attendance improved, suspensions dropped, and the percentage of students who met or exceeded state reading standards jumped from 32 percent to 43 percent. It is very unusual to see any increases on state assessments in the first year of a school improvement process, so that improvement was very impressive. The school was able to maintain that level in reading the subsequent two years but made no further progress. In math the school dropped precipitously the year after Esparza left. No one should be surprised to learn that only a few students were considered proficient in science.

After another year, during which time Esparza served as principal for a high school for Florence Crittendon High School, a school for pregnant students and new mothers, Esparza's wife was hired as superintendent of a district in Oregon.[3] He followed her, happy to be closer to his family in Washington state, and became principal of W. Verne McKinney Elementary School in Hillsboro, a town a few miles outside of Portland. With his prior experiences, he hit the ground running in the summer of 2012. I was lucky enough to visit several times while he was there and once again witnessed the power of the systems he put into place.

STARTING OVER

Hillsboro is the fourth-largest district in Oregon with thirty-seven schools and about twenty-one thousand students. It is home to some large tech companies as well as migrant labor camps, which means that it educates the children of well-off and working-class English-speaking families as well as low-income Spanish-speaking families. The gaps in achievement among those groups are sizable, and the fact that the district had declared that it was taking on the achievement gap made Esparza think he had landed in the right place.

McKinney was a perfect example of the district's need to tackle the achievement gap. It had 460 students, about half of whom were Hispanic, 23 percent learning English, and 70 percent eligible for free and reduced-price meals. The demographics were rapidly changing, with increases in Hispanic and low-income families and decreases in white, middle-class families.

When Esparza arrived, the school was officially considered "satisfactory" in the state's accountability system. If only the performance of the Hispanic students had been taken into account, however, it would have been considered low performing. Twice as many of McKinney's Hispanic students did not meet state reading and math standards as did the white students, and the sizeable but manageable gap in third grade became a chasm in fifth grade. In other words, the longer Hispanic students were at McKinney, the further they fell behind.

Esparza arrived in the summer, so he was able to study the state assessment data not only overall but also by classroom, and he talked with all the teachers individually to get to know them. Among other things, he found out that the previous principal had banned all field trips. "It was all reading, writing, and math," Esparza said. "She took all the fun out of school."

To each teacher, he laid out his vision that any student who was on grade level should grow one year in reading and math; any student who was below grade level should grow at least one-and-a-half years but preferably two. He thought that goal was clear, measurable, achievable, and would, over time, eliminate the achievement gap.

At least initially, Esparza thought the teachers were mostly on board with that goal, and he was hopeful that he would be able to forge the same kind of close partnership with teachers that he had in his previous schools. "One of my strengths is to get people to work together," he told me soon after arriving. But he was concerned that many of the teachers were a bit too quick to claim that the fact that their white students were doing relatively well showed that their practices didn't need to change. They seemed to ignore the fact that their Hispanic students were doing terribly. He knew he would need to help teachers take responsibility for all the students without making them feel under attack. "I need to keep a calm, cool demeanor, but I also have to keep a sense of urgency," he said as a way to explain his approach.

In the meantime, before school started, he addressed the way the building was organized. It had an unusual, 1970s' design in which a large library was at the center of the building. Radiating out were pods of three or four classrooms and an office, each pod housing a grade level with shared space for the teachers to store equipment and meet together as grade-level teams. The general idea of the design was to encourage collaboration among teachers and to make the library the intellectual as well as physical center of the building. Over the previous five or so years, the library instead had been given over to what Esparza called a "maze of offices" for paraprofessionals, special education teachers, and even the parent–teacher organization, with the space divided by portable chalkboards, movable whiteboards, and other makeshift dividers. "The library looks like a shanty town," Esparza told me soon after arriving. "I wouldn't want my kid to be at this school."

He worked with his custodian to remove the screens and curtains that separated the offices, got rid of all the old, mismatched furniture, and ordered new book shelving and comfortable seating. He sought and received a $10,000 grant from the local Kiwanis Club for books. As he ventured deeper into the school, he discovered caches of discarded furniture, cartoon videos, non-educational board games, and hundreds of crayons in closets and in empty and half-used classrooms. That's when Esparza realized how much time was wasted coloring, watching cartoons, and playing board games. "I needed to create time and space for teaching and learning. We don't have to look like *Sanford and Son*," he said. Hidden in the piles of old furniture were boxes of brand new books that had never been unpacked. Over time he and his staff rid the school of the old furniture, televisions, and VCRs and distributed the treasure trove of books onto the library and classroom shelves.

Another area of concern was discipline. He could see from the data that McKinney had had the highest referral rate in the district. So he began the first day with the kind of morning meeting he had instituted at his previous school. The pledge of allegiance ended each meeting, and the "The McKinney Pledge" began it: "We at McKinney Elementary achieve our dreams by being safe, respectful, and responsible. Success comes from HARD WORK. Go Cougars!"

"IF YOU HAVE NO WAY OF MONITORING, YOU CAN'T ADJUST"

Esparza observed the way instruction had been organized, and he started to see why the teachers weren't taking responsibility for all of their students. "The Title I teacher would come and pull the Title I kids," he said, referring to the staff hired under the federal Title I program aimed at ensuring that low-income children learned at the same rate as middle-class children. "The special ed teacher would come and pull the kids with disabilities. Then the English language teachers would pull the kids who were learning English. Classroom teachers were left with a handful of kids, usually the white middle-class kids."

Esparza recognized that this meant that the kids who most needed good core instruction were missing huge chunks of teaching in the name of extra help. It also meant that classroom teachers had very little sense of how all their students were doing. He wanted to change the master schedule immediately, but district-level administrators urged him to spend his first year developing relationships with the staff rather than making fundamental changes. "I could see the systems weren't working and that developing relationships for a year wouldn't fix them," he said.

One of the problems he wanted to address immediately, for example, was that teachers were used to meeting together only once a week, which meant that they didn't have enough time to collaborate. They met in their separate grade-level pod offices, which meant both that the different grade levels were isolated from each other and that they were unable to collaborate with the special educators, Title I teachers, and the English language teachers.

When Esparza suggested teachers use more of their planning periods to collaborate, he faced open rebellion from teachers who refused. Esparza wanted to avoid a complaint to the union, which would in turn trigger a district-level response. So rather than start with changing the systems, he started by demonstrating the need to change the systems to teachers. He did this by making the schoolwide data crystal clear.

In a monthly staff meeting in the large library, he asked every teacher to mark individual student reading achievement with red for below basic, yellow for basic, and green for proficient. He then asked them to put those together as grade-level data on trifold poster boards. He got everyone into a big circle and asked them to open the panels. "The look on staff members' faces ranged from surprise to disappointment," Esparza said. "Over 75 percent of our students were either red or yellow. Staff members were bewildered and couldn't believe their school was so behind."

This was his opportunity. First, he proposed that staff meet in the library and not in individual pods. Second, he asked staff to work an extra 30 minutes on the day they met together in exchange for leaving 30 minutes early on Friday. Third, he asked that reading and math academic data be put on Excel spreadsheets with color coding so that fellow teachers, including the English language, Title I, and special educator teachers, all had access to it.

After the staff agreed to all three proposals, the school started building a system in which all faculty members were able to monitor how students were doing and adjust instruction. "It's all about monitoring and adjusting," Esparza said. "But if you have no way of monitoring, you can't adjust."

As time passed, Esparza found that some teachers were openly expressing disbelief that all children could master grade-level work. He needed something to show that all students could meet standards. He found an online math program that allowed students to work at their own pace to master particular parts of the math curriculum, provided tutorial lessons, and also provided detailed reports on what students had mastered—or failed to master. Esparza convinced his district-level leaders to allow him to purchase the program and offered it in the before- and after-school program. A few teachers saw the power of the supplemental program and put it to use. As students began mastering two-digit multiplication and other math standards, teachers became convinced it was useful, and it eventually became a schoolwide system.

In the morning meetings Esparza began talking about the school collectively solving one million math problems. This meant that on average each student would have to correctly solve more than two thousand online math problems during the year. He considered that goal more than doable and that reaching it would provide students the kind of practice they needed. He also promised every student a school T-shirt with the McKinney pledge on the back if they mastered the math facts appropriate to their grade. Esparza expected everyone to pass timed tests in order to be able to wear the shirts on Fridays—including staff, custodians, secretaries, and himself. Kindergarteners needed to count to one hundred to get the T-shirt; third-graders needed to know their multiplication tables through 10×10. In the hallways and after the morning meeting, kids began begging him to give them math problems so that they could show they could add $4 + 4$ or multiply 6×8. Parents started asking him if they could buy their children the T-shirts, and he would say, "No, they have to earn it."

Reading posed a similar problem to math: there was no way to consistently monitor how much students were reading and whether they were improving. He instituted Reading Counts, which—similar to Accelerated Reader—provides quick comprehension tests for thousands of books so that teachers and principals could monitor students' reading levels and progress. The books in the library were color coded so that students could choose books at or just above their reading level.

He was not confident that either program was closely enough aligned with the state tests to be predictive of how students would do, but both provided immediate feedback and, as he said, a computer "never tires. It doesn't give you sighs, or faces of frustration." He set a goal that students should read 100 million words as documented by Reading Counts.

To ensure students had access to these computer-based systems, Esparza bought $50,000 worth of new computers, including an iPad for every teacher—and was amused at how impressed the teachers were that he was able to do so. The previous principal had never been able to keep the school current with technology. With control over the school's Title I budget, Esparza had simply not replaced two Title I aides who had left the previous year and used the money for computers, paper, and other materials. For the first time, teachers weren't finding themselves short of paper and saw that their school could keep up with the more affluent schools in the area of technology. His judgment was that those particular Title I aides hadn't been able to boost achievement, so he didn't think the school was losing anything by not replacing them.

He began following the results of the math and reading programs and highlighting students who were making progress and those who weren't, looking both at students individually and by class, and asking teachers to make plans for those students who were not progressing. This effort was part of ensuring that teachers didn't simply assume that some students were the responsibility of the Title I teacher or the special education teacher. "I told them that all the kids' scores are theirs."

Esparza was also working on developing the leadership capacity within the school. He had no dean or assistant principal, but the first year he had inherited a half-time reading coach and a half-time math coach. Together, he said, they did not add up to one school leader who could reliably help teachers improve instruction. He spent the first year on the lookout for someone in the district he could bring to the school.

He found Jennifer Robbins, who was working in the district office but had been a very well-regarded teacher and was eager to help McKinney and work with Esparza. She was interested in eventually becoming a principal and saw him as someone she could learn from. He figured out a way to hire her for the next year, and even though officially she wasn't a full-time instructional coach, that is how she functioned. As such, she sat in teacher meetings helping them study the state's standards and look at the progress of each of their students individually as well as collectively and think about what else to try.

Despite the fact that he hadn't been able to make all the changes he wanted that first year, when the state assessment results came back during the summer, the school had made the greatest growth of any school in the district. Proficiency rates had not changed much, but students were closer to proficiency than they had been, and for the first time the English language learners were ahead of the English language learners in the rest of the state.

Esparza was happy to see that the computer math and reading programs he had brought in mapped onto the state assessments pretty well; that is, 90 percent of the time it was possible to use their results to predict how well students would do on the state assessment, which meant that teachers began to develop more confidence in them. "You should be able to find some system—either MAPS or Moby Max or Accelerated Reader or Lexile levels—that you can look at as a teacher, a student, or a parent on a continual basis to know if you are on track to meet state standards. Otherwise, it's a hope and a prayer."

Because the school's students had gained so significantly, Esparza felt he had gained enough credibility with the staff to make changes in the master schedule whereby Title I aides and special education teachers would "push in" their services to classrooms more often and pull out students less. The teachers, Esparza said, resisted this. "They say, 'we don't have time to train all these people to help us in the classroom.' So I said, 'Give it to us. We'll train them.' So now I have their lesson plans and assignments, and I can really see what they're asking of the kids. And they're really just at the first level—they are not at higher-order questions."

By that, he meant that the questions teachers were asking students were more simple recall ("What was the character wearing?") rather than more complex analytical questions ("Why did the character act that way? What else could he have done? If he had, what might have happened?

What evidence from the text can you cite for that opinion?"). He and Robbins started talking about how to increase the rigor of instruction.

Esparza also used his success to fend off two efforts by the district that he thought threatened the school's ability to progress. The first was an effort to have McKinney institute a dual-language program. Esparza had initially been enthusiastic because he found compelling the research saying that dual-language programs are helpful in helping all students succeed. However, over time he saw that the district wasn't planning on investing in the training or materials indicated by the research.

District officials were also pushing him to "split" classes, meaning divide classes into multigrade classrooms containing two grade levels in order to lower overall class size. Although split, or combination, classes are common in many schools, Esparza feared it would undermine efforts by teachers to study grade-level standards and work together as grade levels to improve instruction. "We'd rather have large classes than split classes," Esparza said. Resisting the district's importuning on these questions cost a lot of time and effort, but it bought him some much-needed support from teachers.

In addition, this was a year when the state was in the process of instituting enormous changes. "I have a new teacher evaluation system, a new set of standards, and a new student management system," Esparza said. "That's a lot of change." Also, the state had only one more year of the old assessments before it was moving to a new assessment, Smarter Balanced, which had been developed by a consortium of states to assess whether students were meeting Common Core State Standards. "That's not going to be a fifty-mile-an-hour ball," Esparza said. "It's going to be more like a one-hundred-mile-an-hour ball."

Over the year, Esparza and Robbins continued to refine the basic systems of helping teachers collaborate on instruction, developing systems of information for students, parents, and teachers, and building the motivation of students.

"It got so I could go to any classroom and say that one key word, 'Success?' and the students would say 'Comes from HARD WORK. Go Cougars!' and they would settle down and get to work." Esparza thinks that in general not enough attention is paid to building students' motivation. "It's not about giving them trinkets and toys," he said, referring to some popular behavior management systems that reward students for good behavior which, he said, don't take into account "the desire of kids to be part of something."

When the second year's results were published, McKinney had not just made more progress than any other school in the district, but also had improved its proficiency scores sufficiently to actually move up an entire level on the state's rating system. For the first time, students at McKinney were doing better than their counterparts in the rest of the state. That is to say, higher percentages of McKinney's white, Hispanic, and economically disadvantaged students were meeting state standards than Oregon's white, Hispanic, and economically disadvantaged students.

Esparza was elated with the results, and he and Robbins made plans for a summer school program to focus on Science, Technology, Engineering, and Math (STEM).

"INSUFFICIENT CAUSE"

Then Esparza's career imploded.

He allowed a visitor who claimed to be from an anti-bullying program to visit the school. It turned out the visitor was a convicted criminal, and when a local television station began asking the district about the visit, the district reported Esparza for misconduct to the state's Teacher Standards and Practices Commission. He resigned rather than see the school be embroiled in a controversy that he feared could impede its progress.

"In hindsight, I should have vetted the visitor more carefully," Esparza said. He later learned that there is a software system that scans drivers' licenses and runs them through a quick criminal background check. "I highly recommend that all schools invest the few thousand dollars to keep your school safe from possible threats," he told me.

The state commission eventually dismissed the allegations, saying in its official letter that there was "insufficient cause to charge you with misconduct" and issued him a four-year administrative license. But by that time Esparza had left education altogether and was working to manage his parents' land so that it would provide them with a retirement income.

To me, this seems like a minor lapse was allowed to derail a thirty-two-year career. Esparza always welcomed visitors to his schools. I can attest to that personally because I was the beneficiary of that openness; the first time I showed up at Granger High School, he had no idea who I was. It appears he allowed into the school someone who probably shouldn't have been there, but no one ever alleged that the visitor was left alone with children or was ever unsupervised.

I can't help but think that if Esparza had not been an outsider to the district—or if he had been more compliant with district desires—he might not have been so quickly discarded.

I haven't been able to visit McKinney since Esparza left, but I have kept tabs on the school's results and kept in touch with Jennifer Robbins, who was determined to keep the school's progress going.

She ran the school's summer STEM program, which she and Esparza had envisioned, during which students—among other things—built two rowboats. She said students were so engaged in the STEM projects that the outside teachers who taught in the program couldn't tell which students ordinarily posed behavior problems.

With the arrival of a new principal, Robbins was concerned that he would not understand the effectiveness of the systems and want to remove them. It would be easy for the school to lose its momentum. "We were changing from an experienced leader who had implemented a vision to a leader, new to our district, with a high learning curve."

To his credit, the principal let Robbins continue many of the processes Esparza had started. By then, the teachers had become convinced that the monitoring systems he had put in place helped them track the progress of their students. "The staff has a heavy buy-in," she said. In addition, most teachers were now used to taking responsibility for all their students, and they had seen for themselves that even students who they didn't think initially could achieve could work hard, learn, and master the state's standards.

Robbins told me, "Staff members have said that they appreciate the energy and systems that Ricardo implemented—even the ones who were reticent at first."

At the end of the 2014–2015 school year, she said, "This year has taught me which systems could be maintained after a great leader has left. I am proud to say that I have been able to maintain our data systems and the extension of the school day and year programs."

That summer Robbins once again ran the school's STEM summer school and spearheaded the application for the school to become the district's first Title I STEM school, a designation it gained the following year.

When the results from the state assessments came back for the 2014–2015 school year, the school had not just continued its academic progress, but was among the state's top improvers, according to an analysis done by the *Oregonian*.[4] Because of the new assessments, the state had suspended its report card grades that year, but Robbins said she thought if it hadn't, the school might have jumped another rating.

The new assessment was Smarter Balanced, which Esparza had predicted would hit the school like a hundred-mile-an-hour-fast ball. But McKinney held its own, with its overall performance more or less matching the state's performance. And its student groups did better than their counterparts in the state, so, for example, 51 percent of McKinney's economically disadvantaged students met or exceeded state reading standards, compared to 40 percent in the state; and 64 percent met state science standards compared to 56 percent in the state.

FIGURE 6-1

McKinney Elementary School English Language Arts, 2015

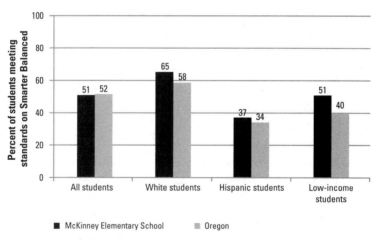

Source: Oregon Department of Education

McKinney still couldn't be considered high performing, but those three years had made a real difference. I was happy to see the team from McKinney honored for its progress at the National Title I Conference in January 2016 as a Distinguished School.

SYSTEMS TO NOTE

- Systems to monitor progress toward grade-level standards in both reading and math.
- Systems to communicate students' progress—or lack thereof—to teachers, students, and parents.
- A master schedule that permitted collaboration and a system to ensure that specialists could collaborate with classroom teachers.
- A system to build motivation and a desire to work and succeed among students.

A FEW OBSERVATIONS

- Key to Esparza's work has always been a deep belief in the capacity of children. But he didn't operate on belief alone. Rather, he focused on developing systems to improve instruction and give teachers and students clear and immediate feedback on their progress.
- It is very easy for a traditionally organized school's systems to go awry. For example, what seemed like a system to help students who were behind by pulling them out for extra help at McKinney actually undermined their ability to receive core instruction and diminished the sense of responsibility teachers felt for their progress. This system was allowed to continue for years because the school wasn't used to studying data to see what was working and what wasn't.
- Esparza's continual cheerleading helped enlist students' hopes and dreams for themselves—and rekindled teachers' confidence and enthusiasm, all of which was part of improving the schools in which he worked.

- As student achievement improves, teachers begin to see more possibilities for their students and start to believe in the efficacy of their actions.
- Extra time is important; before school, after school, and summer school are all important in helping students who are behind catch up.
- Perhaps a key lesson is that districts can undermine the work of school leaders.

CHAPTER SEVEN

Could There Be "Unexpected Districts" as Well as Unexpected Schools?

In *It's Being Done* (2007), I wrote that I deliberately didn't talk much about the district context of unexpected schools because many of the schools' leaders had told me of difficult relationships with their districts. These school leaders said that they just wanted to operate their schools in ways they knew were powerful and hoped their district leaders would leave them alone. Some even said that they were ostracized within their districts, with many of their fellow principals treating them like pariahs because of their successes. One said, laughing, "They say our students have a 'strain' of brilliance, as if it were an illness."

It has struck me that the attitude of those principals is comparable to that of good teachers who try to ignore the incoherence of the schools they are in by closing their doors and teaching as well as they can, hoping their principals will just leave them alone. Although those teachers' actions are completely understandable, that kind of isolated teaching is ultimately harmful to the field and to students—first, because it keeps expertise locked up in a classroom, inaccessible to colleagues and other students; and second, because no individual teachers—no matter how powerful—can possibly know enough to teach all the curriculum to all their students. That is to say, individual teachers will never be as good by themselves as they would be in a school coherently organized to support teaching and learning.

I have come to believe that the same is true for schools.

That is to say, schools operating in isolation lock up the expertise they have developed and lock themselves away from the expertise of others. As a result they can't possibly be as good as they could within a district coherently organized to support teaching and learning. Still, just as most teachers can't determine the systems within which they work, neither can most schools. School leaders determine the culture and systems within which teachers teach; district leaders develop the culture and systems within which schools operate. And those cultures and systems can either support or undermine teaching and learning.

At the most basic level, district leaders appoint principals. And, as we saw with M. Hall Stanton Elementary in Philadelphia and Graham Road Elementary in Fairfax County (chapter 5), no school—no matter how strong and set up for future improvement—can withstand the appointment of a principal not able or willing to continue the culture and kinds of systems that made that school successful.[1]

Districts undermine schools in plenty of other ways, though, even if they do appoint principals who know what they're doing. In the preceding chapter, I provided a couple of examples of district officials undermining improvement by following political and personal predilections rather than the best research and craft knowledge. This is another way of saying that principals can fix schools all they want; they won't stay fixed in an incoherent district.

I should acknowledge school districts are complicated. If schools are masses of moving parts, districts are infinitely more complex. And the research base of knowledge about how to improve districts is not nearly as large as that about improving schools. That doesn't mean there are no district leaders to learn from. As with schools, we can look for outliers, see what it is they do, and decide whether it makes sense to learn from them.

The following begins an effort to do so. I consider this work to be in the very early stages and don't want to in any way exaggerate its importance. But to me, the Indian River School District in Delaware is a prom-

Frankford, was if anything higher performing than Frankford had been, putting it at the top of the state in terms of achievement.

At East Millsboro, which I also wrote about in *It's Being Done*, I again saw system after system that was designed to ensure that all students learned a great deal—professional learning communities, professional development, and master schedules designed to make the most of every minute of the day. Gary Brittingham had been there for twenty-five years, and the school ran like a clock. One of the things he said has stuck with me all these years: "If you can predict who is going to have some difficulty, we in the business should figure out some way to help that child."

His statement recognized that educators know ahead of time that some kids will arrive behind and that the point of schools is to help them anyway. It was a powerful acceptance of professional responsibility.

Over the years I kept in touch with Sharon Brittingham, and she shared with me her distress that Frankford was no longer as high achieving as it had been when she was principal. Finally, however, she reported that the district had appointed a new principal, and she was confident the school was back on track. Under CharLynne Hopkins, it indeed did get back on track, and by 2014, in a new building and under the new name of John M. Clayton Elementary School, it received the National Blue Ribbon award for its achievement.

In other words, when the school went off-track, that was a temporary condition, not a permanent one. When I talked with Sharon, she told me that she had great confidence in the district's systems and that as worried and upset as she had been about Frankford, she never thought it would be allowed to completely fall apart.

Under her urging, I started to look at the district's statistics a little more closely.

Indian River is a district that has undergone enormous demographic shifts. From 2004 to 2016, it went from about eight thousand students to about ten thousand students, fueled mostly by what sometimes seemed to be the recruitment of entire villages and towns in Mexico and Central America by the local poultry factories, one of which is located right next to the district's central office. When the wind blows, feathers blow into any open windows. Many of the district's new families are low income;

many speak little or no English. In 2013, 60 percent of the district's students qualified for free and reduced-price meals. Since then the data on free and reduced-price meals has gotten less reliable; the state now reports that the district's free and reduced-price meal rate is only 40 percent, but the superintendent, Dr. Susan Bunting, says that that number is way off and that 60 percent is much closer to reality.

The kinds of demographic shifts Indian River underwent over the last decade would normally throw a district completely off track. And yet Indian River—slowly and unevenly but most definitely—improved during that decade. In 2014, the last year under the old assessment system, Indian River's elementary schools as a whole were at the top of the state; the middle and high schools, slower out of the gate, had also improved and were about even with the level of secondary schools in the rest of the state.

When Smarter Balanced replaced the old state assessments in 2015, it demonstrated that Indian River and Delaware still have a lot of work to do, but in many grades and subjects, Indian River still outperforms the state. So, for example, 67 percent of Indian River's fifth graders met state standards in English language arts, compared to 56 percent in the rest of the state. Forty-five percent of the district's fifth graders met state math standards compared to 38 percent in the state. At eleventh grade, the district is almost at the level of the state but not quite. Graduation rates exceed the state for every demographic subgroup except Hispanic students. That is, 85 percent of all students graduated in 2015, including 83 percent of African American and low-income students. That number compares to 84 percent overall in the state, 81 percent of African Americans and 70 percent of low-income students. Only 77 percent of Hispanic students graduated in Indian River, compared to 82 percent in the state.

For a high-poverty district to improve as its student population is getting poorer and more diverse seems to me to be worth paying attention to, so I traveled back to Indian River to try to understand what it was doing as a district. What I found was a superintendent who was thoughtful and systematic in how she approached district improvement. She brought the same kinds of thinking about systems that I have seen in unexpected schools. As well, I found principals, assistant principals, and teachers who spoke of coherence and support from the district that I haven't heard often.

FIGURE 7-1

Indian River School District Graduation Rates, 2015

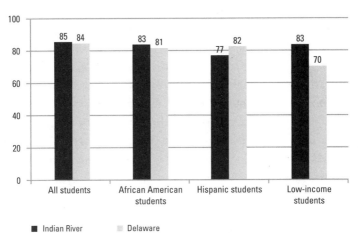

Source: Delaware Department of Education

To begin with, Bunting states as the vision of the district that "every student will improve." In some ways, it is a modest vision—it does not say "every student will excel," for example. However, its very modesty ensures its wide acceptance. It doesn't call for an enormous leap of faith but rather draws on the professionalism of educators to ensure their students will improve. The vision was brought to the district by the previous superintendent, Lois Hobbs, for whom Bunting served as curriculum coordinator before succeeding her in the job in 2006.

"Everyone agrees that students should improve," Bunting says. But, she added, the key is not just having a vision but having a comprehensive system of monitoring whether every single student does in fact improve.

Monitoring starts in classrooms where each teacher monitors the growth and improvement of each student. Teachers meet regularly with their grade levels and their principals to look at that monitoring data and discuss what more can be done to move students forward, with systems to provide help to faltering students and enrichment to excelling students.

This system is then mirrored at a district level. Bunting formally meets twice a year with each principal to talk through what the principals are doing to help their teachers improve. What professional development have they arranged? What peer walk-through processes are they leading? What books are they studying? How are they incorporating complex questioning and close reading in their buildings?

During those meetings, principals go through a "balanced report card" that lays out goals for each school. "And I hold them accountable for each piece," Bunting said. But just as the principals in unexpected schools see their role as being much more than formally monitoring the work of teachers regularly in classrooms and collaboration meetings, Bunting meets with principals many times each year about myriad topics, goes to their schools at least three times a year to visit all classrooms, and has regular conversations with each of them via text, e-mail, and phone.

In addition, she randomly pulls 20 percent of the teacher evaluations to give feedback to the principals to ensure that they are holding to the standard that all students will improve. When she thinks that principals aren't pushing hard enough on teachers to read key research or engage students in complex questions, she expects them to improve on those measures.

Principals at the district's sixteen schools, in turn, are expected to look at samples of student work to ensure that teachers are expecting enough of their students.

"It's a comprehensive system," Bunting says. This continual monitoring is in some ways high pressure, particularly on building leaders. But it is accompanied by the kind of support Bunting expects principals to provide teachers.

"We have had a leadership institute for the last eleven years," Bunting says. "As our teachers get professional development opportunities, our principals are learning—and implementing what it is we're learning as our own professional learning community." Once a month all the principals meet together as a group, and once a month the principals at each level (elementary, middle, and high school) meet to talk through the issues that face them.

Sharon Brittingham, who now works with principals throughout the state through the University of Delaware, remembers when she first began as principal. Principal meetings, she said, were "day-long meetings where you checked off agenda items and you went out of here thinking, 'Oh, my gosh.'" Over time, she said, "We started having meaningful conversations and sharing best practices. We read books; we talked about books and the implications for our buildings. We would learn something and take it back to our buildings and reflect on that in the portfolios we did. We [became] a learning organization."

This professional support of building leaders reflects Bunting's idea that, as she says, "Teachers can have all the training and know what should happen, but it's the building leader who leads instruction—and I insist that principals be learning leaders of their buildings."

Principal of Millsboro Middle School Renee Jerns says, "What we do with [Bunting] trickles down to the kids. So the kids in my school have their own little professional learning communities . . . where they go in a corner and teach each other. They keep their own data cards. . . . So we model for them that we're constant learners and look at data. They're learners. We're learners. We're all in it together."

In addition, as teachers participate in their professional learning communities, principals are on the watch for leadership potential. Teachers who are interested in leadership opportunities are brought into a districtwide administrative development program where the superintendent and other central office directors teach classes about instructional and managerial leadership and the issues faced by the district. When he was still principal of Sussex High School, Jay Owens said of the administrative development program, "It's comforting when you're getting to know the upper-level administration from the ground floor as a teacher or an assistant principal in an environment that isn't as rigid as the work environment can be." Meeting with the superintendent, the director of finance, the director of curriculum, and other district leaders allows aspiring leaders to have, he said, "kind of a test drive. So when you're in the driver's seat, you have a good relationship with these people and you don't feel nervous picking up the phone and talking to them or going to them."

Owens now works in the district office as the director of special services, which points to the kind of systematic leadership development Indian River has, allowing it to hire from within rather than looking for leadership from outside the district.

Indian River isn't the only district that I've run across that works on building comprehensive systems of monitoring, support, and leadership development, and I'm sure there would be many more if we were to look in a systematic way for outlier districts.

SYSTEMS TO NOTE

- Monitoring of individual student growth by teachers.
- Monitoring of individual teacher growth by school leaders.
- Monitoring of individual principal growth by district leaders.
- Recruitment and training of leaders at the school and district level.

A FEW OBSERVATIONS

- In unexpected schools, the expectation is always that all students will meet or exceed state standards. Indian River has a more modest goal that all students will progress; but it keeps things moving, enlists teachers' sense of professionalism, and has helped Bunting avoid battles about beliefs.
- There is a parallel to be drawn between the systems of scheduling, monitoring, support, and accountability in unexpected schools and in Indian River School District—and, I suspect, other well-organized districts.
- The district focused its attention first on building the knowledge and skills of elementary school teachers and thus building the knowledge and skills of their elementary students. But it is now focused on secondary schools, and I have hope that we will see even more progress on that front in future years.

CHAPTER EIGHT

Marshaling the Power of Schools

I can't remember a time when I didn't think of public schools as the crucible of American democracy, founded to provide all children—independent of family circumstances—with a solid education that prepares them for future citizenship.

Yet the ones I attended as a child, the ones I observed as a newspaper reporter, and the ones my children went to did little to sustain that idealistic vision. Until I began actively searching out unexpectedly successful schools, the schools I experienced seemed to be organized around random acts of education, replicating inequity rather than disrupting it.

Many years ago I tried to express my dismay in a newspaper column by referring to the sloppy organization of schools. My inelegant characterization elicited an angry letter from a teacher who said that he and his colleagues were working harder than anyone had a right to expect and that I shouldn't call anything they did sloppy. Of course, he added in a burst of honesty, some teachers sat in class reading the newspaper rather than teach—but most teachers were working incredibly hard.

I asked this teacher what his school did to ensure that the students with the newspaper-reading teachers were learning what they needed to learn, and he responded: "Nothing. They're screwed."

And that's what I had meant by sloppy. This teacher's school was firmly in the tradition of being organized around isolated and idiosyncratic classrooms. As such, students could not depend on the support of the entire school but instead had to depend solely on the efforts of individual teachers. And if teachers read the newspaper in class, so be it. At the same time, teachers could not depend on the support of the entire school, and even the hardest-working teachers saw their efforts weakened and dissipated. This point was driven home to me in subsequent conversations with my correspondent, who was frustrated that his work wasn't having the effect he had expected to have. Like many of his fellow teachers who enter the field with great optimism and idealism, he left a couple of years later, angry and disappointed.

Since then, I have spent more than a decade seeking out and learning from what I call unexpected schools—high performing and rapidly improving schools with large percentages of students of color and students from low-income families.

These schools have restored my belief that it is possible for schools to act as crucibles of democracy, providing a solid education and opportunities to students independent of their family circumstances. I no longer *think* it's possible; I *know* it is possible because I have seen such schools. Those schools are not just good places to be a student but also are satisfying places to work. In unexpected school after unexpected school, I have heard teachers and other staff members say that—although they work incredibly hard—they love their jobs because they know they are making a difference in children's lives within a supportive environment that they often describe as "like a family."

So what is it that these teachers do to be so successful? If you were to go to these schools, you would see, well, schools. They don't *look* all that different from other schools. In many ways, they look very traditional, and they operate under the same rules and policies as other schools in their districts and states. And yet their results indicate that they are doing something very different. So what is it?

I have spent a lot of time puzzling that question through. Certainly, it is critically important that these schools have leaders who feel a moral imperative to do what is right for kids and who spend a good deal of time understanding the research evidence about teaching and learning. The previous books I have authored and coauthored have made that clear. But at a certain point in the last few years, I realized I had not paid enough attention to the bread-and-butter work of the schools that allows them to get the results they do.

I think back many years to when I was writing a newspaper column about schools in Prince George's County, Maryland. I noticed that one of the high schools had been recognized as having more African American AP test-takers and passers than any other high school in the region, and I wanted to know what they were doing. When I visited the school, I thought the first thing the principal would do would be to tell me his AP teachers were amazing and give me a tour of the classrooms. He did eventually, and the teachers were great, and I was able to watch kids extract DNA from fruit and discuss the American Revolution.

The *first* thing the principal did, however, was take me into the office of his assistant principal, who was in charge of the school's schedule, point to a giant chart on the wall-sized whiteboard that showed when every class in the school was taught at what day and time and by whom and where, and say something to the effect of "*that's* the reason for our success."

I look back on that moment as the beginning of my education about systems. I wasn't ready to hear it yet, so much of what the assistant principal subsequently told me went over my head. The chart, as any school person can say, was the master schedule of the school. I remember listening to the assistant principal tell me that it was built around the semester-by-semester expansion of AP classes and how he had hand scheduled hundreds of AP students to ensure they got all their classes. As he walked me through the chart to show me how he juggled all the priorities of the school to focus on giving more students the opportunity to be exposed to and master advanced material, it began to dawn on me that the master schedule was a concrete expression of the school's values.

My education has continued through more than a decade of visiting unexpected schools. In each one, teachers and leaders have talked about the issues their very vulnerable students bring to school and the systems they have put into place to address them, from master schedules to counseling groups.

These schools not only put in systems but also continually evaluate them so that they can continue and expand the ones that work or change or jettison those that don't. Here's a small example of what I mean. The teachers and leaders of Elmont Memorial High School (chapter 3) noticed that their ninth graders were having difficulty making the transition from middle to high school. They used the master schedule to set up a "ninth-grade academy" in which groups of students would share teams of teachers who could collaborate on how to teach individual students. "It worked. For a while," said John Capozzi, the former principal. That is to say, for a year or two ninth graders were more successful than they had been. They started slipping again because new issues had emerged. Elmont changed the schedule again.

THE SCIENTIFIC METHOD IN ACTION

In a sense this is the scientific method in action: See a problem. Analyze the cause of the problem in the light of established research. Develop a hypothesis for how to solve it. Set up a system to reflect the hypothesis and measure results. Assess to see if the system solved the problem. If it solved the problem, see if there is a way to strengthen or extend the solution. If it didn't solve the problem—that is, if the system failed—that is not a cause for blame. Rather, it is part of the learning process en route to developing another hypothesis and another system. As such, the work is never done. As Capozzi said, "If you think you're done, it's time to get out."

By focusing so closely on the systems underlying their work, educators are able to develop a professional distance and look at success and failure dispassionately rather than as a personal win or loss. The ability to examine evidence dispassionately is important because education in many ways is a very personal field, and anything that helps teachers and leaders evaluate what they are doing instead of defending how much they love a particular practice or lesson plan is important.

By the way, I don't mean anything fancy by the term *system*. I am simply using the term to mean how schools organize things to get stuff done.[1]

I understand that this is not a story of romance or drama. I venture to say that there will never be a movie about the leadership team of Artesia High School developing the master schedule or the instructional teams at Graham Road and West Gate Elementary Schools following protocols for their data meetings.

Despite the lack of drama, it is in these prosaic systems, continually monitored and examined, in which the success of unexpected schools can be located.

All of this is to say that *unexpected schools have marshaled the power of schools as institutions by establishing systems that:*

- *make visible the expectation that all students will achieve and make such achievement possible;*
- *develop leaders who help build, monitor, and evaluate the systems;*
- *support the building of relationships;*
- *improve instruction by opening up practice in ways that help expose the expertise that exists within classrooms and schools and then helping others learn from it. Specifically, this means systems that support teachers in*
  - *focusing on what students need to learn;*
  - *collaborating on how to teach them;*
  - *assessing frequently;*
  - *using data to find patterns in instruction.*

Let's examine these points one by one.

1) UNEXPECTED SCHOOLS HAVE MARSHALED THE POWER OF SCHOOLS AS INSTITUTIONS BY ESTABLISHING SYSTEMS THAT MAKE VISIBLE THE EXPECTATION THAT ALL STUDENTS WILL ACHIEVE AND MAKE THEIR ACHIEVEMENT POSSIBLE. In many ways, the educators in unexpected schools embody what Stanford psychologist Carol Dweck calls a growth mindset.[2] Sergio Garcia, principal of Los Angeles County's Artesia High School (chapter 1), summed it up for all of them: "It's not about talent; it's about effort."

Yet when Garcia first encountered Artesia High School, he found a school that through its systems had not only made visible the expectation that most students would not achieve but also enforced that expectation very efficiently. That is, he found a school that had reserved advanced work for only a few students and had much lower-level instruction for the rest. Diane Scricca, former principal of Nassau County's Elmont Memorial High School (chapter 3), found the same thing when she saw that mostly white students were in advanced classes and mostly

African American students were in remedial classes. For students at both schools, the message was clear: Some kids are smart, and they get to talk about great literature, wrestle with historical dilemmas, learn foreign languages, and study knotty mathematical and scientific problems; other kids are not-so-smart and do remedial work that never seems to remediate. That is to say, they do low-level work that never helps them access higher-level work but just keeps them busy and bored. When they become angry at how their time is wasted, they are prime candidates for suspension and expulsion.[3]

To address this problem, Garcia and Scricca both used one of the most powerful systems they had available to them: *the master schedule*. Garcia acted immediately, even before school started his first year, to get all students who had been scheduled for consumer math, pre-algebra, and general math into Algebra I. Because he knew that students who hadn't really mastered arithmetic were going to be in trouble, he scheduled those students who were behind into a second class that provided additional help and scheduled after-school tutoring for students who needed it.

Note that having *a system of extra support* is key. Many schools and school districts in the last decade have declared their intention to get every eighth grader into Algebra I, knowing that that is a gateway to higher math and thus college preparation. And yet many did not build in a system of support that would allow those students who hadn't fully mastered arithmetic to be successful in algebra. That meant hordes of students have failed to master Algebra I, to the frustration of students and teachers all over the country.

As Garcia says, "You can have all the expectations in the world, but if you don't have systems of support, it doesn't mean anything."

Scricca did much the same thing as Garcia, although she took a somewhat more gradualist approach. Beginning with the seventh grade and working her way up through the grades, she eliminated all classes below the level of honors, or college preparatory. She still needed a system of support, though. To get that, she scheduled the seventh- and eighth-grade English and math teachers so that they had four sections of one class, meaning that they had only one set of lessons to prepare. For their fifth class she scheduled the teachers to teach a support class in which they previewed for struggling students the vocabulary and background they would need for those lessons, anticipating the obstacles and misunderstandings students might have. "We didn't wait for them to fail. We gave them the support they needed ahead of time," Scricca said.

Note that Garcia and Scricca knew—from research and their own experience—that until struggling students develop a growth mindset, they see coming in for extra help as an expression of failure and are reluctant to come after school. Knowing that, Garcia and Scricca built the extra help into the school day, making it a requirement rather than optional.

This approach is emblematic of all the unexpected schools—students are expected to master high-level class work—and the schools have systems to improve core classroom instruction that we'll get to in a minute. The educators in the schools are well aware that even the best classroom instruction can't always compensate for gaps in vocabulary, background knowledge, and organizational wherewithal. Rather than lower standards, the schools build a system of mandatory additional support for students.

When Elmont Memorial High School faced an issue with an influx of new high school students, many of whom were unprepared for the rigor of Elmont's classes, Scricca set up another system whereby students were required to attend Saturday "Welcome Academy" classes that alternated, week by week, between English and social studies, and math and science. In those classes the teachers previewed the work students would be doing in the coming weeks, helping them learn the necessary vocabulary and background knowledge and anticipating misunderstandings. Most students and families probably knew that Scricca couldn't legally require students to attend on Saturday, but they came anyway. And new students did much better than before the Welcome Academy was established.

Elementary schools, of course, have different kinds of master schedules because students generally have only one classroom teacher rather than six or seven. Many elementary schools have rather simple master schedules built around the key questions of when kids go to lunch, recess, and "specials," meaning art, music, and so forth.

Sometimes elementary schools allow the specials teachers to build the schedules, resulting in fragmented instructional schedules. Sometimes master schedules are simply arranged in ways that they have always been arranged. One of my favorite examples is that when Deb Gustafson walked into Ware Elementary, which I wrote about in *HOW It's Being Done*, she found that the master schedule was arranged so that every class had fifteen minutes to go to the bathroom in the morning and afternoon, thus using up half an hour a day—ninety hours a year—that could otherwise have been used for instruction. Not only was it a huge time waster, the master schedule assumed that all kids needed to go to the bathroom at the same time. Needless to say, she changed the schedules immediately and set the policy that students would go to the bathroom when they needed to rather than when the schedule said they should.

In fact, pretty much the first thing all the unexpected school leaders did when they arrived in their schools was to redo the master schedule. In elementary schools, the goal was always to provide uninterrupted blocks of time for instruction for students and collaboration of teachers. Some of this rescheduling is about using the resources available to the school in the most efficient way. So, for example, when Molly Bensinger-Lacy arrived at Graham Road (chapter 5), she immediately changed the master schedule so that the specialists who could help with reading instruction—the special educator, the English for Speakers of Other Languages (ESOL) teacher, the reading specialist, and so forth—were in classrooms during the appropriate time. This meant that teachers were no longer in charge of when they would teach reading and when math; they had to teach reading when the master schedule said. Because the supply of resource teachers was limited, it also meant that reading was taught throughout the day so that the specialists could move from grade to grade. As a result, teachers couldn't teach reading only in the morning, which is when many prefer to do so. Such an incursion into the isolated, autonomous, idiosyncratic classroom was not welcomed by all of the teachers, who were used to arranging their instruction. However, it was necessary if all students were to get the support they needed to master grade-level standards.

As in the unexpected secondary schools, the elementary schools build in additional support in what they usually call *systems of interventions*. So, for example, Craig Gfeller (chapter 5) used the master schedule to build in 20 minutes a day for students to get individual extra help for anything they were struggling with—three days in their classrooms and two days in specialists' rooms. Similarly, Ricardo Leblanc-Esparza (chapter 6) scheduled half-an-hour a day for "flex time," which allowed students to get extra help. I have seen schools—particularly schools where many students are learning English—in which an entire hour a day is scheduled for intervention. The reason is that, as Bensinger-Lacy says, "You lose your motivation when you're failing and no one is available to help you."

As unexpected schools become more successful, they become more focused on students who have already mastered the material taught in their classes. When the data indicate they have students who are advanced, they build *systems of enrichment* to provide additional challenges for them.

Both the systems of interventions and systems of enrichment require systems of assessment data, but we will get to them in point 4.

Systems of discipline become another way to make expectations visible. Unexpected schools expect students to meet high standards, including high behavioral standards, but they consider discipline to be another form of educational support rather than punishment. This is a key distinction, and one that is being grappled with now in national conversations about racial and class disparities in school disciplinary actions.

I should say, before going any further, that students who bring weapons or hard drugs and thus endanger other students are suspended and expelled in unexpected schools. In this, they are like other schools.

Such incidents are highly unusual, though. The much more ordinary disciplinary issues of talking back, often called defiance and insubordination, are seen as opportunities to build relationships, develop motivation, and make clear that students are expected to achieve in unexpected schools. For example, Ricardo Leblanc-Esparza used misbehavior as a way to connect back to students' ambitions. "Didn't you tell me you wanted to be a nurse?" he would say. "Is this behavior going to help you? No? Let's get back to work." Every time he met with a student and the student's parents in his office about a disciplinary matter—actually, whenever he met with them—he began by going over the data—what the student's reading and math levels were, what these levels should be, and what they were going to do about that. The academic needs of students were his focus; discipline was a means to fulfill those needs.

The emphasis in unexpected schools is always on making sure students do not lose instructional time whenever possible. Even those students who are suspended will sometimes be brought back to school for a particularly important lesson.

All the unexpected school leaders understand that many disciplinary problems can be traced back to feelings of failure or feelings of boredom, both of which can be fixed by improved instruction. Kennard Branch, when he began at Garfield Prep (chapter 5), said he first focused on improving instruction because he thought it would handle 80 percent of the discipline problems. He was a little overoptimistic, but not much: discipline problems dropped 70 percent as instruction improved. To address the remaining discipline issues, he developed a system of direct behavioral support to teachers. Garfield Prep is down to having just three or four students who remain what he calls "high-flyers."

Unexpected school leaders and teachers also know that some disciplinary issues emerge because their students have suffered trauma or are dealing with difficult situations. Such students often have hair-trigger reactions to failure and feeling disrespected, and unexpected school educators believe that helping them learn to cope and deal with those feelings is part of their job.

"If you can overcome a crisis in your life; if you can overcome poverty; if you can overcome crime; if you can overcome any obstacle in your life, you become a stronger person," says Jennie Black, about whom I wrote in *HOW It's Being Done*. "So we need to see poverty and we need to tell children, 'You are strong enough to handle this. Now what do we need to do to help you get to that next level?'"

Ricci Hall at Claremont Academy (chapter 5) works to help students get a handle on their anger and inappropriate behavior. A very typical situation in schools—including Claremont—is that a teacher remonstrates with a student in a way the student believes is unfair. He or she objects, the discussion escalates, and the teacher finally throws the student out of class for insubordination. Hall works with students to find better ways to have handled the situation. Then quietly, without undermining the teacher's authority, he works with the teacher on ways that the teacher might be able to de-escalate the next situation, helping students feel respected and act in more respectful ways.

Framing discipline as another way of educating students is a recognition that many schools have a tradition of treating students in ways that are disrespectful. When Deb Gustafson arrived at Ware Elementary, she told teachers that the only thing she would ever discipline them for is being disrespectful to a student. When teachers objected that they were themselves disrespected by students, she said that children's behaviors are a direct reflection of what is occurring around them in the school. "The school is so powerful; this is why you can have children from very dysfunctional homes demonstrate respectful behaviors at school. Respect gathers respect."

Similarly, Hall says repeatedly, "Teacher culture drives student culture."

For this reason, a student who was, in Scricca's words, "wigging out" in the hallway one day could easily have been suspended in another high school. Instead he became a "special project" for her and other staff members who made a point of checking in with him, making sure he was okay, and seeing if he needed anything. "The leaders establish the expectations for teachers," said Scricca. "You are expected to love every kid—even the unlovable ones—and I'm going to show you how by my doing it. Every single day."

Similarly, every day Debbie Bolden, principal of Gilliard Elementary (chapter 4), checked the backpack of a student who threatened to kill his teacher earlier in the semester, asks him how he's doing, gives him a big hug, and tells him to have a good day.

When students' behavior requires more help than can be provided by instructional staff, unexpected schools work to bring in whatever outside help is available. When they can, they have social workers on staff who work to help students manage their emotions. At Malverne High School, I heard from many students who credited social worker Joseph Aquino with helping them deal with their anger and distrust to focus on academics. It took Gilliard Elementary School years, but it finally was able to get public mental health professionals assigned part-time to the school; George Hall Elementary (chapter 4) physically took students to psychiatrists who would be paid by families' Medicaid funds until they were able to set up a video link so that students could have check-ins with their psychiatrists remotely.

All of these examples illustrate that unexpected schools don't write off any student, no matter how difficult their circumstances or their behavior. They say all students can achieve, and then they build the systems that can make that happen.

Master schedules and systems of discipline are two of the most powerful systems all the unexpected schools use to enforce beliefs about student capacities, but they aren't the only ones. They all have *systems of recognition* that work to enforce the idea that all students can achieve.

Schools must be very careful about what these systems of recognition are because many, in an attempt to incorporate the idea of growth mindsets, lost their way by recognizing unproductive effort rather than achievement. In fact, the trend became so alarming that Carol Dweck wrote an article in *Education Week* in 2015 to try to get educators to stop praising effort.

> Recently, someone asked what keeps me up at night. It's the fear that the mindset concepts, which grew up to *counter* the failed self-esteem movement, will be used to *perpetuate* that movement. In other words, if you want to make students feel good, even if they're not learning, just praise their effort! Want to hide learning gaps from them? Just tell them, "Everyone is smart!" The growth mindset was intended to help close achievement gaps, not hide them. It is about telling the truth about a student's current achievement and then, together, doing something about it, helping him or her become smarter. [4]

From what I have seen, unexpected schools have not fallen into the trap that Dweck worries about. They know that students need to feel successful and that success builds upon success. So, particularly when they are first starting, these schools might find ways to recognize accomplishments that fall short of actual achievement. They might, for example, recognize task completion—that is, something completely within the control of students—such as keeping their writing journal for an entire week, meeting their Accelerated Reader goal, or attending a Saturday support class.

Making this effort is just a stepping stone to recognition for successful, productive struggle with academic work. Ricardo Leblanc-Esparza would give a school T-shirt that could be worn on "Spirit Fridays" to any students who mastered the math facts appropriate to their grade level. Kindergarteners counted to one hundred; third graders mastered their multiplication facts, and so on. The adults—the teachers, secretaries, janitors, and even Esparza—had their own math tests to master in order to get the T-shirts. It took some time for some of the students—and even for all the adults—but eventually they all got their T-shirts. They wore them proudly, knowing that the shirts were symbols of actual accomplishment and that they were part of collectively raising school achievement.

When Artesia High School first began recognizing academic achievement, Sergio Garcia realized he had to first make recognition safe when a student stuffed a celebratory T-shirt into his backpack saying that he could get beaten up for doing well in school. "We needed to do mass recognition," Garcia said. So he and the other leaders worked out a system to recognize both absolute achievement and progress together. If a student went from F to F+, that was recognized, on the grounds that sooner or later improvement would get the student to achievement. Now most students at Artesia are recognized for real accomplishment, even if it is only a small step toward achievement.

By recognizing both absolute achievement and improvement—in classrooms and schoolwide—students taste the rewards of success and begin to see the results of hard work. They themselves begin to see that they can get smarter. A senior at Imperial High School, which I wrote about in *HOW It's Being Done*, said, "At other schools, [you hear], '*there* are the smart kids.' Here, we're *all* the smart kids." That's one of the most striking things I ever heard a student say.

Unexpected school leaders often have to bring their teachers along on this question of high expectations. "They have come through a system," Vincent Romano (chapter 2), principal of Malverne High School, told me. "There were the regular kids, the honors kids, the AP kids. A lot of teachers were the AP kids. We're still challenging the idea that it's the haves and the have-nots." And so, unexpected schools develop a *system of professional development that focuses on setting high expectations for all children.* Sometimes that means leading book studies of Carol Dweck's work, case studies of successful high-poverty schools, or reviews of research such as books by Robert Marzano or John Hattie; sometimes it means visiting schools with similar demographics that are more successful; sometimes it means having teachers get training from Jeff Howard's Efficacy Institute or from Learning Forward, one of the country's key professional development organizations.[5] The leaders know that changing beliefs about the nature of intelligence is not easy and truly happens only when teachers see improved instruction help unexpected students achieve. But the leaders' belief in the power of education means that they believe teachers, too, can learn and become more expert.

Just as they have systems of recognition for student achievement and progress, these leaders similarly recognize teachers for the achievement and progress of their students. "When teachers are holding students to high expectations and we see success—that is celebrated too," said Vincent Romano. "I think after years of this, many of our teachers think they can walk on water!"

A couple of other systems seem obvious and yet they need to be mentioned:

- *A system of organizing the physical space of schools to maximize learning.* Educators in schools rarely have the chance to weigh in on the actual architecture of their buildings. For the most part they are stuck with whatever they have. But they can make the most of what they have. A school that is dirty, disorganized, and where teachers and classes are scattered higgledy-piggledy is a clear signal to children and their parents—and to teachers and other staff members—that not much is expected of them and there isn't a lot of support to help them achieve. As Craig Gfeller says, the condition of the building is a "metaphor" for the expectations in the building. This is why almost every unexpected school leader spends time initially making sure the building is clean and well organized. School maintenance people are considered to be leaders of the physical environment of learning and are thus part of the educational experience students have—that is to say, they also play an important role in educating students. In the unexpected schools I've been in, they are clearly proud of that role. They encourage students to do their best and are sometimes even mentors for them. In other words, school maintenance staff members are treated with the same kind of respect and authority and responsibility as any other member of the team and have the same level of expectations set for their work. This is true for everyone—the cafeteria workers, the school secretaries, the teachers' aides—everyone.
- *A system of organizing supplies and materials to maximize learning.* As I was writing this conclusion, I mentioned the issue of supplies to a couple of principals, and I heard stories I had never heard before. For example,

Molly Bensinger-Lacy told me that when she arrived at Graham Road Elementary, the school had a locked book room that had a huge inventory of books that teachers could request but couldn't browse. Since they weren't allowed in, they didn't even know what was there. Many had spent their own money to buy classroom books or used old and inadequate basal readers. Bensinger-Lacy had to order the teacher's aide who was in charge of the book room to allow teachers in. "There were lots of tears," she said. Similarly, Sergio Garcia said when he arrived, teachers weren't allowed in the photocopy rooms. He had to order the secretarial staff to allow the teachers to make copies.

Another leader who has taken the job of principal in a low performing school heard complaints from teachers that they didn't have the materials and supplies they needed when she first arrived. When she toured the building, she found an entire closet of Scotch tape, the result of years' worth of standing orders to the district. After she gave away as much tape to the other schools in the district as they would take, she still had half a closet's worth. She immediately reviewed the supply list requested of the district to make sure that it reflected what kids actually need for learning.

It isn't hard to ensure that teachers have the materials and supplies they should have. All of these schools get federal Title I dollars which can be used for materials and supplies. But making sure the resources are used properly takes leaders who pay attention to ensuring that teachers and students have what they need in order to teach and learn. When leaders don't pay attention, it is yet another signal to kids—and, even more pointedly, to teachers—that they are on their own.

2) UNEXPECTED SCHOOLS HAVE MARSHALED THE POWER OF SCHOOLS AS INSTITUTIONS BY ESTABLISHING SYSTEMS THAT DEVELOP LEADERS WHO HELP BUILD, MONITOR, AND EVALUATE THE SYSTEMS (AND IN THE PROCESS BUILD THE NEXT GENERATION OF SCHOOL LEADERS). Setting up a system is relatively easy. But the power of a system doesn't come from setting it up; it comes from implementing the system faithfully and then evaluating to see if it accomplished the goal it was intended to accomplish. If it did, it needs to continue or intensify; if it didn't, it needs to be adjusted or abandoned. That evaluative process first requires monitoring to ensure

that the system is being followed and to gather the appropriate data to see if it's working.

Monitoring is the part few people want to do because it's—well, quite honestly—it's kind of tedious.

When Esparza set up a system at Granger High School to ensure that every student's family was met with and their help enlisted by a student's advisor, he had to monitor to make sure that those meetings actually happened. That task involved receiving a piece of paper from every advisor reporting on the student conferences and keeping the resulting contracts available in case they were needed. None of that requires overwhelming effort, but it requires a system of monitoring that involves a certain amount of tedium. Similarly, someone had to continually monitor attendance and update the poster Granger had in the hall stating which students owed time to the school because of unexcused absences. Unless you can see a direct line from that system to helping students achieve at higher levels, it is hard to maintain the enthusiasm for that kind of continual monitoring.

Principals are the obvious people to monitor many of the systems in a school. But schools address far too many issues for principals to be the only monitors.

At this point leadership throughout the school—what Harvard University's Richard Elmore calls "distributed leadership"—comes into play. Teachers, counselors, assistant principals, school secretaries, cafeteria managers—everyone is a leader in some way in unexpected schools, and they all build and monitor systems. At Artesia High School, this monitoring even extends to the master schedule, which is built every year by the thirteen members of the leadership team, including department chairs who represent the interests of the teachers in their departments. In addition, Artesia High School has thirty-nine schoolwide systems—they call them "campaigns"—that the entire faculty have agreed to. All those systems have to be monitored, but most of them, such as the way data is used and displayed in classrooms, or ensuring that students are writing across the curriculum, are monitored by the teachers themselves. "They all get rolled up and go past my desk where I review them, but I don't do the initial monitoring. They have internal accountability," says Sergio Garcia.

I should note that some of Artesia's systems originate with teachers and are adopted even against Garcia's wishes. This happens for two reasons:

first, because teachers' professionalism and expertise are respected and valued; and second, because Garcia knows that any mistakes that are made in setting up systems will be caught in the monitoring and evaluation process. That is to say, if systems don't solve the problems they were intended to solve, the monitoring process ensures that fact will be noticed and the evaluation process ensures it will be changed or jettisoned.

Every unexpected school has its own version of a leadership development system that helps build the evaluative capacity of everyone in the building. So, for example, Scricca regularly had her cabinet members observe a videotaped lesson together and share what observations they had and what commendations and recommendations they would give to teachers. This process helped all the leaders in the school understand not only what instruction should look like but also what help and support leaders were expected to offer teachers.

This leadership development is part of what Deb Gustafson of Ware Elementary says gets the flywheel going. That is to say, the initial effort to marshal all the systems of a school to help students be successful is enormously time- and energy-consuming, somewhat like the energy needed to get the flywheel of a machine going. Once it's in motion, though, it almost keeps itself going.

For example, when Molly Bensinger-Lacy was principal of Graham Road Elementary School, she sat in on every grade-level collaboration meeting to ensure teachers stayed focused on instruction and didn't get sidetracked into discussing logistical issues such as chartering buses for field trips. At a certain point, when the grade-level leaders she had trained and developed had taken control of monitoring and adjusting the systems, "I realized I wasn't needed there anymore." She kept track of the meetings by reviewing the agendas and notes from the meetings, but she no longer needed to attend the meetings in person.

The leadership development process in unexpected schools has another powerful effect beyond ensuring individual coherent schools, and that is in developing leaders to make change in other schools. In this book I identified Kennard Branch and Craig Gfeller as the "next generation" to highlight how this process works, but actually there are many more examples of leaders who got their training at unexpected schools. Elmont Memorial High School alone has been the training ground for principals, assistant superintendents, and superintendents across Long Island. I didn't write much about her in this book, but Deb Gustafson at Ware Elementary is a one-woman principal preparation program, responsible for the hiring and training of more than half the principals in her district and others in that part of Kansas. Similarly, over the past decade Artesia High School has produced almost a dozen principals and assistant principals who are scattered around southern California, part of a deliberate process on the part of Sergio Garcia to "replicate what's happening here so it doesn't die with the school."

Large national conversations are going on about how we can get more of the school leaders we need. It seems to me that one way is for unexpected schools to incubate them. That's not a quick fix. But it may be an enduring one.

3) UNEXPECTED SCHOOLS HAVE MARSHALED THE POWER OF SCHOOLS AS INSTITUTIONS BY ESTABLISHING SYSTEMS THAT BUILD RELATIONSHIPS. In *HOW It's Being Done*, I identified five key processes that all unexpected schools shared. We'll get to the other four in a minute, but one of them was "build relationships."

Identifying this process is a simple way to talk about what in many ways is a complex subject. A great deal of research indicates that how students feel about school and their teachers is key to how much and how well they learn. This is particularly true for students who are experiencing academic failure or some kinds of difficulties in their home lives.

Educators in unexpected schools build systems to ensure that students—particularly students who are having some kind of problem—develop strong relationships with at least one adult in the school who expresses confidence in the child's ability to overcome obstacles and meet high standards—and offers help and support. For example, almost all the schools have as many after-school classes and programs as they can possibly pay for in order to help build student connections to the school both through fun activities and through their relationships with the teachers who lead clubs and sports. When Scricca arrived at Elmont, she found a school where almost every sport was coached by someone who did not teach at the school. It took her six years, but over time she convinced teachers that it was important to students that they have nonclassroom connections with teachers—and that teachers have that connection to students.

Similarly, Artesia High School developed a full complement of after-school activities to make the school an "oasis" for students and a "center for the community."

It is when schools have a particular worry about a student, however, that their systems really kick in. At many schools, anyone who has a concern about a student can request some kind of team meeting at which the power of the school is mustered. The team might ask for a staff member—anyone from the maintenance engineer to the school secretary—to volunteer to check in with the student every day, have lunch once a week, or make some other regular contact and report back to the team how the student is doing. If that isn't sufficient, further resources will be drawn on—counselors, social workers, outside mental health services—whatever is necessary. For example, Malverne High School has a plan in place for every student about whom the school has concerns. That means that a staff member serves as a mentor who helps guide the student into appropriate help and support and into activities he or she might enjoy. When Kesha Bascombe (chapter 2) realized that teachers needed ready access to that information so that they would know what was going on, she built an Excel sheet that teachers can consult if a question about a student arises.

Ware Elementary, which has a great deal of student turnover because it sits on an army base, had a worry about how new students would quickly integrate into the school. The school developed a system in which new students are assigned to a group of student leaders who sit with them at lunch, explain the school's rules and culture, and go to recess with them. (By the way, being chosen as a student leader is part of the system of recognition, in this case for students' good school citizenship.)

This process doesn't work only for students; new teachers at Ware are also assigned a group of teacher leaders who perform the adult version of integrating newbies into the school culture. This example points to the fact that student connections aren't the only relationships being built. Relationships among teachers and staff are also systematically cultivated both through the processes of collaboration and through systematic social events to build collegiality. For example, before schoolwide events such as concerts and plays, faculty members at Artesia have dinner together;

at other schools grade levels, departments, and entire faculties regularly have breakfasts and barbeques.

The point is that building relationships is seen as important, and because it is important, it is not left to happenstance.

4) UNEXPECTED SCHOOLS HAVE MARSHALED THE POWER OF SCHOOLS AS INSTITUTIONS BY ESTABLISHING SYSTEMS THAT IMPROVE INSTRUCTION BY EXPOSING THE EXPERTISE THAT EXISTS WITHIN CLASSROOMS AND SCHOOLS AND THEN HELPING OTHERS LEARN FROM IT. The way unexpected schools improve instruction is by incorporating four processes, all of which have the effect of opening up practice. I discuss them in great detail in *HOW It's Being Done*. I won't repeat everything I said there, but briefly the four processes require the following:

- *A laser-like focus on what students need to know.* This means that teachers must all have a clear, shared idea of what standards and curriculum students are expected to master and what they need to know to a great level of specificity. For example, if students are expected to analyze primary-source documents, teachers agree on a clear definition of what primary-source documents are and which ones they will use to teach students the topic they are addressing.
- *Collaboration on how to teach it.* No one single teacher can possibly know all the curriculum, the pedagogy, and all the students well enough to teach all students all they need to know. If every student is to master standards, teachers must be able to draw on both available research and the combined craft knowledge and expertise of all the teachers in their school—and sometimes in their district or region.
- *Frequent assessment to see if students learned it.* Students need timely, accurate feedback on what they are learning; teachers need timely, accurate feedback on what they are teaching. Abundant research indicates this kind of feedback is key to student achievement, and assessments help provide it.[6] Not every assessment needs to be a paper-and-pencil test; assessments can be exit tickets, oral presentations, even classroom discussion. But they need to be frequent. While many assessments should be made by teachers to provide immediate, focused feedback on daily lessons, regular outside assessments are also necessary to ensure

teachers' instruction is on the right track. Those outside assessments should be aligned to the standards and curriculum schools are expected to teach, and students and teachers should be able to see all the questions and answers so that they can get all the feedback information they need from them. That is not where we are right now with state assessments, but it is what we should aim for.

- *Using data to drive instruction.* Unexpected schools use assessment data in two ways:
  - to see which students learned whatever was taught and need enrichment and which students didn't learn it and need extra instruction;
  - to find patterns in instruction, by which I mean looking for which teachers, which grade levels, which departments, which groups were doing better to expose expertise and learn from it.

The most powerful conversation that can occur in any school is when one teacher says to another, "Your kids did better than mine. What did you do?" And that conversation can happen only when teachers are looking at data from the same assessments of the same subject matter given at roughly the same time. That means that teachers need to agree on what they are teaching when.

Put together, the preceding four processes are what drive the improvements in instruction in unexpected schools.

All of these processes require systems to ensure that they can and will happen.

One of the simplest ways for schools to open up classrooms to expose expertise is to literally open them up so that teachers can observe each other's classrooms. Even simply seeing each other's classes can be eye-opening for teachers. More powerful than random observation, however, is teachers observing their colleagues employing effective practices or teaching specific content in which they are particularly expert. But, as teachers all over the country can attest, this requires master schedules that support classroom observation—which often includes coverage of classrooms, either by other teachers or leaders or substitute teachers. And that requires having a system to ensure that whoever is covering the class is knowledgeable and skillful enough to continue the learning in that class. The reason is that, as Valarie Lewis of P.S. 124, which I wrote about in *HOW It's Being Done,* has said, "No one has the right to waste a student's time."

Observation, though valuable, is only the beginning. Unexpected schools employ deep collaboration to improve instruction. For example, at Claremont Academy teachers have slowly begun developing "collaborative lesson plans" to gather the knowledge and expertise of their colleagues in providing their students with what they call "powerful learning experiences." At Elmont and Malverne, teachers collaborate with their colleagues and their department chairs to deepen their lessons and make them as powerful as possible.

At all unexpected schools, teachers meet together regularly as teams or departments to collaborate. Often they need more time than the standard hour-or-so-a-day planning time most teachers have as part of their contracts, and that requires some creativity on the part of leaders, either in finding substitute teachers to cover classes, or some other solution. To give just one example in detail, at Graham Road, Molly Bensinger-Lacy and her team realized that the way the master schedule operated, grade-level teams were not able to collaborate with the specialists—the ESOL teachers, special educators, and the reading specialist—and so instruction was not as coherent as it needed to be. So she cobbled together an hour a week for each grade level from kindergarten through fifth grade.

The way this worked was that she and the teachers agreed that in exchange for leaving fifteen minutes before the end of the contractual day one day a week, teachers, including the specialists, would meet one day in the library at the beginning of the contractual day—that is, at 7:45 a.m.—for seventy minutes during the time that was normally allocated for setting up their classroom and for the first fifteen minutes of school. During that fifteen minutes of school time, their classes were covered by teaching assistants and the counselor and art, music, physical education, and Spanish language teachers, who would collect homework, hold morning meetings, and begin the instructional day.

During their meetings, teachers studied standards, planned lessons, planned and analyzed results from common assessments, discussed professional literature, or focused on a problem of practice they had identified and collaborated about how to incorporate the research and expertise they had developed in a systematic way. This was a powerful way to improve instruction, but it required several systems to be in place:

1. The master schedule and coverage schedule for classroom teachers, as well as an arrival schedule for staff monitoring the arrival of buses, students arriving on foot and by car, and breakfast that didn't conflict with the coverage schedule.
2. An established morning routine of students entering the school and classrooms ready to learn.
3. A cadre of trained teachers' aides and "specials" teachers who understood the morning routines and knew how to move instruction along so that students' time wasn't wasted.
4. A system of communication between teachers and the staff members who covered their classes.
5. A system of data collection and analysis to enable teachers to identify significant problems of practice.
6. Carefully built protocols to ensure that that 70 minutes of collaboration accomplished the goals of improving the knowledge and expertise of teachers so that instruction would improve.
7. Team calendars that scheduled discussion of standards, lesson planning, and follow-up assessments to match curriculum pacing guides.

This example gives just a sense of the underpinnings of one way to improve instruction. But let's face it: This requires a level of rather tedious management; it would have been very easy to simply say it was impossible. But Bensinger-Lacy—like the other unexpected school leaders—knew that her students needed expert instruction to learn to high levels, and that required that teachers continually improve their knowledge and skills. And that required the kind of collaboration that couldn't be accommodated in a normal schedule.

A particularly powerful system for improving instruction is the *teacher observation and evaluation system*, and unexpected schools all take it very seriously. Teachers and classroom instruction are the heart of unexpected schools, and the observation and evaluation systems unexpected school leaders employ are designed to help them improve. Principals think of themselves as head teachers, and as such are not only teachers' bosses but also their teachers and resources. None of them have the same exact system, but they all have ways to ensure that principals and other leaders are in classrooms regularly and meet with teachers to talk about instruction. In fact, they often schedule their time in classrooms and in collaboration meetings first, making the rest of their job fit in.

Just as unexpected schools ensure that additional systems of support are in place for students who struggle, they ensure that additional systems of support are in place for teachers who struggle. "There's an analogy between students and teachers," said Scricca. "My best leaders were my best teachers—because they taught the teachers."

If a teacher is having a particular problem with classroom management or with teaching a particular topic, for example, that teacher might be teamed up with another teacher who is more expert in that area. I've seen teachers double up their classes to take advantage of a particular teacher's expertise. Or the more expert teacher—or reading or math specialist—might teach model lessons while the other teacher is present to observe.

Professional development doesn't stop, however, when a teacher isn't struggling. All teachers have more they can learn or areas in which they can become more skillful. There is simply too much for a teacher to know to think that any teacher can possibly be expert in all areas. Having this clear understanding removes the stigma of imperfection. No one is expected to be perfect. But all teachers are expected to be moving forward and improving. It is there that the evaluation system comes in, in unexpected schools. Teachers who refuse to participate in the processes that lead to improvement are considered to be real drags on the school and come under increasing scrutiny, with more observations and more intense conversations about what their plans are for each one of their students and what lessons they plan.

Sometimes teachers under that kind of scrutiny rise to the challenge and engage more productively in collaboration and improve their classroom instruction. When they don't, they often leave of their own accord, worn out by the expectations and unwilling to face the continual disappointment of their fellow teachers. But if they don't leave on their own accord, the leaders consider it their responsibility to counsel them out of the profession. "Strong school leaders must be able to honestly say, 'I would place my own child in this classroom,'" Deb Gustafson of Ware Elementary said. "The removal of ineffective teachers is some of the most difficult and time-consuming work of a school leader, but also some of the most important."

Unexpected school leaders try to hire people who share their vision that all students will achieve. They provide a great deal of help and support to teachers to help them achieve success, but at a certain point they will give up on a teacher in a way they will not give up on a student. Then these leaders do not engage in simply passing along teachers they think are harmful to other schools, a practice widely known as "the dance of the lemons." They do the work to document teachers' failings and either counsel them out of the profession or fire them. Leaders do that because they feel a responsibility to children to ensure they get a good education.

The systems many of the unexpected leaders have for observation and evaluation have been disrupted by the new evaluation systems that have been put in place in most states. The New York State evaluation system was one part of why John Capozzi left as principal of Elmont Memorial High School. He felt he had been relegated to a mere manager of an evaluation system that, in his eyes, did teachers—and thus students—a disservice. Most of the unexpected school leaders have found ways to make the new evaluation systems work for them, but doing so has required quite a few contortions. The rigid evaluative guidelines many states have mandated are an attempt at a kind of workaround around the rather weak principal corps. But evaluative checklists will never substitute for deep professional knowledge and expertise. That is to say, there is no workaround. We need leaders who understand how to lead improvement.

FINAL WORDS

People who haven't hung around schools much might be puzzled by the essential argument that I am making in this book, which is that schools should be organized in ways to ensure that all students learn a great deal.

They might think: "They're schools! What else would they be organized around?"

Yet many pressures on schools pull away from a coherent set of organizational practices that enable high achievement. The most significant pressure is the traditional way schools have been organized around isolated, individual, autonomous practice. To overcome the institutional inertia that protects individual classrooms requires a deep belief that all students are capable of achievement and an equally deep belief that it is the responsibility of adults in a school to work together to ensure that students succeed. This question of belief in students' capacities is at the core of unexpected schools. If teachers and other educators don't believe in their students' abilities, they are more likely to simply keep going with what they're doing. That doesn't mean, by the way, that they're not working hard. Most educators are working very hard. But if they don't believe their students are capable of developing their abilities, they will be reluctant to go that extra distance to learn what more can be done and change what they are doing, and then keep changing in response to new students, new colleagues, new standards, new assessments, new content, new research, and new technologies in the light of research and the craft knowledge that has been developed by expert educators.

I am not saying that educators should jump on every bandwagon or "innovate" simply for the sake of innovation. But they need to keep the end result—student achievement—in mind and continually think about what else can help to reach it, setting up systems, monitoring, and adjusting.

This is the type of innovation I have seen in unexpected schools, and if educators can make schools work for poor children and children of color, then they can make them work for all children. After all, unexpected schools have all kinds of strikes against them: they often have shamefully scarce resources and the low prestige that comes from serving the students they serve. And yet they have marshaled the collective power of schools as institutions in ways that make them enormously successful.

We should acknowledge that educating all children is difficult work and that most educators don't yet have the knowledge and expertise necessary. But that doesn't mean the knowledge and expertise don't exist. As Sergio Garcia says, "This isn't rocket science. It's doable."

But it's doable only if we pay great attention to what it takes to create and sustain these schools. And it's doable only if educators believe their students are capable of achievement and are willing to do the systematic, thoughtful, creative—and occasionally tedious—work necessary to provide it.

Notes

INTRODUCTION

1. Kenneth Leithwood, et al., "How Leadership Influences Student Learning," The Wallace Foundation, 2004, http://www.wallacefoundation.org/knowledge -center/Documents/How-Leadership-Influences-Student-Learning.pdf.
2. Richard Elmore, "Building a New Structure for School Leadership," The Albert Shanker Institute, 2000. http://www.shankerinstitute.org/sites/shanker /files/building.pdf.
3. Ibid.
4. A recent contribution to this literature is Sean Reardon, "School District Socioeconomic Status, Race, and Academic Achievement," Stanford University, 2016, https://cepa.stanford.edu/content/school-district-socioeconomic -status-race-and-academic-achievement.

CHAPTER ONE

1. Hearings on Elementary and Secondary Education Act of 1965, 89th Cong. (1965, January 26) (statement of Robert F. Kennedy, Senate Committee on Labor and Public Welfare).
2. Trends in Academic Progress, Reading 1971–2012; Mathematics 1973–2012, Institute for Education Sciences, National Center for Education Statistics, http://nces.ed.gov/nationsreportcard/subject/publications/main2012/pdf /2013456.pdf.
3. In the interests of full disclosure, I should say that I have quite a few ties to the American Federation of Teachers. For example, its magazine, *American Educator*, has excerpted my books, and I have written articles for *American Educator* and its other publication, *American Teacher*.
4. I relied on California's Data Quest website, which has a treasure trove of information about schools, though it is a rather clunky format. http://dq.cde .ca.gov/dataquest/.
5. For an explanation of API, go to the California Department of Education. http://www.cde.ca.gov/ta/ac/pa/cefpsaa.asp.
6. The FBI website has a good deal of information about the Hawaiian Gardens gang, including this press release from 2009: https://archives.fbi.gov/archives /losangeles/press-releases/2009/la052109.htm.

CHAPTER 2

1. Amy Stuart Wells, et al., "Divided We Fall: The Story of Separate and Un-equal Suburban Schools 60 Years After Brown v. Board of Education." (The Center for Understanding Race and Education [CURE], Teachers College, Columbia University, 2014).
2. AP data, which is not publicly available, was provided by Vincent Romano, principal of Malverne Senior High School. All other data came from the New York State Department of Education's school report cards.

CHAPTER 3

1. Diane B. Scricca, Albert J. Coppola, and Gerard E. Connors, *Supportive Supervision: Becoming a Teacher of Teachers,* (Thousand Oaks, CA: Corwin Press, 2004); Diane Scricca and Mary Ellen Freeley, *Become a Leader of Leaders: Raise Student Achievement* (Lanham, MD: Rowman and Littlefield, 2014).
2. Daniel Willingham, *Why Don't Students Like School: A Cognitive Scientist Answers Questions About How the Mind Works and What It Means for the Classroom* (San Francisco: Jossey-Bass, 2010); *When Can You Trust the Experts: How to Tell Good Science from Bad in Education* (San Francisco: Jossey-Bass, 2012); and *Raising Kids Who Read: What Parents and Teachers Can Do* (San Francisco: Jossey-Bass, 2014).
3. Carol Dweck, *Mindset: The New Psychology of Success: How We Can Learn to Fulfill Our Potential* (New York: Ballantine, 2006).

CHAPTER 5

1. For a description of the work of the Efficacy Institute, see chapter 3, "How Malverne Became Malverne."
2. Many states use student growth percentiles as a way to provide more context for proficiency rates. Here is how the Massachusetts Department of Education explained its SGP in 2011:

> "Achievement scores answer one thing: how did a student fare relative to grade level standards in a given year. Massachusetts Comprehensive Assessment System (MCAS) student growth percentiles add another layer of understanding, providing a measure of how a student changed from one year to the next relative to other students with similar MCAS test score histories."

The document further explained it this way:

> "Percentiles are commonly understood values that express the percentage of cases that fall below a certain score. For example:
>
> • "A student with a growth percentile of 90 in 5th grade mathematics grew as much or more than 90 percent of her academic peers (students

with similar score histories) from the 4th grade math MCAS to the 5th grade math MCAS. Only 10 percent of her academic peers grew more in math than she did. or

- "A student with a growth percentile of 23 in 8th grade English language arts grew as well or better than 23 percent of her academic peers (students with similar score histories) from the 7th grade ELA MCAS to the 8th grade ELA MCAS. This student grew less in ELA than 77 percent of her academic peers."

For the full explanation, see "MCAS Student Growth Percentiles: Interpretive Guide," Massachusetts Department of Elementary and Secondary Education, March 2011, http://www.doe.mass.edu/mcas/growth/InterpretiveGuide.pdf.

3. "Emerging Practices in Rapid Achievement Gain Schools: An Analysis of 2010–11 Level 4 Schools to Identify Organizational and Instructional Practices that Accelerate Students' Academic Achievement," Institute for Strategic Leadership and Learning. Developed for the Massachusetts Department of Elementary and Secondary Education, February, 2012.

4. For an explanation of "growth mindset," see chapter 8, "Marshaling the Power of Schools."

5. Japanese lesson study was first brought to the attention of American educators as a result of the administration of the Third International Math Science Study, a standardized test given to samples of fourth and eighth graders around the world. For more, see James W. Stigler and James Hiebert, *The Teaching Gap* (New York, NY: Free Press, 1999).

6. Richard DuFour, et al., *Raising the Bar and Closing the Gap: Whatever It Takes* (Bloomington, IN: Solution Tree Press, 2010).

7. The teachers were wrestling with an issue that has been identified as a key math misunderstanding and has been the topic of great discussion by mathematicians and experts in math pedagogy, such as Deborah Ball of the University of Michigan.

CHAPTER 6

1. For what I consider to be a brilliant study of low performing schools, see Charles Payne, *So Much Reform, So Little Change: The Persistence of Failure in Urban Schools,* (Cambridge, MA: Harvard Education Press, 2006).

2. Years later the two would write a book together: Ricardo Leblanc-Esparza and William Roulston, *Breaking the Poverty Barrier: Changing Students' Lives with Passion, Perseverance, and Performance* (Bloomington, IN: Solution Tree Press, 2012).

3. During this time Esparza and his wife published a book together: Ricardo Leblanc-Esparza and Kym Leblanc-Esparza, *Strengthening the Connection Between School and Home* (Bloomington, IN: Solution Tree Press, 2013).

4. Betsy Hammond, "Report Cards on Oregon Schools Show Which Produced Exceptional Gains, Anemic Growth," *Oregonian,* October 15, 2015, http://www.oregonlive.com/education/index.ssf/2015/10/report_cards_on_oregon_schools.html.

CHAPTER 7

1. The Wallace Foundation has taken on the task of seeing what it would take for districts to be very intentional and smart about recruiting, training, hiring, inducting, and supporting principals. See http://www.wallacefoundation.org/knowledge-center/school-leadership.
2. Some of the material in this chapter is adapted from Karin Chenoweth, "Teachers Matter. Yes. Schools Matter. Yes. Districts Matter. Really? How?" *Kappan,* October 2015.

CHAPTER 8

1. As with so many things, I am indebted to Molly Bensinger-Lacy for helping me with this definition.
2. With a "growth mindset," people believe that their most basic abilities can be developed through dedication and hard work. It stands in contrast to what Dweck calls a "fixed mindset," which holds that intelligence and talent are inborn and immutable. Carol Dweck, *Mindset: The New Psychology of Success: How We Can Learn to Fulfill Our Potential* (New York: Ballantine, 2006).
3. For an interesting sociological study of how this dynamic works in an ethnically diverse but wealthy high school, see Amanda E. Lewis and John Diamond, *Despite the Best Intentions: How Racial Inequality Thrives in Good Schools* (New York: Oxford University Press, 2015). The authors let educators off the hook by blaming parents for the large achievement gaps, but their book demonstrates quite clearly how the systems in a school can enforce the vision of low expectations.
4. Carol Dweck, "Carol Dweck Revisits 'the Growth Mindset,'" *Education Week,* September 22, 2015, http://www.edweek.org/ew/articles/2015/09/23/carol-dweck-revisits-the-growth-mindset.html?qs=carol+dweck.
5. Examples include Robert Marzano and John Brown, *A Handbook for the Art and Science of Teaching* (Alexandria VA: ASCD, 2009); and John Hattie, *Visible Learning: A Synthesis of Over 800 Meta-Analyses Related to Achievement* (New York: Routledge, 2009).
6. After conducting a meta-analysis of more than eight hundred meta-analyses of educational research, John Hattie concluded that providing fast, accurate feedback to students is one of the most effective educational practices available to teachers. John Hattie, *Visible Learning* (New York: Routledge, 2009). Accurate feedback is also one of the key principles that emerged from more

than a century of study into how people learn, principles that were nicely summarized into a quick cheat sheet for educators by cognitive scientist Daniel Willingham and educator Paul Bruno. Deans for Impact, *The Science of Learning* (Austin, TX: Deans for Impact, 2015), http://www.deansforimpact.org/pdfs/The_Science_of_Learning.pdf.

Acknowledgments

A little while ago I realized that I may have been in more high performing high-poverty schools than anyone else in the country. I'm perfectly willing to cede that title if someone has a stronger claim, but I don't know anyone else who has had as a job visiting schools that I have called "unexpected"—that is, schools that are high performing or rapidly improving and have large populations of students of color and students from low-income families.

I have been enormously lucky to be employed to find and visit such schools by The Education Trust, a national education advocacy organization that works to improve the academic achievement of all children, but particularly children from low-income families and children of color. It has often been called the "conscience of American education."

Many years ago Ed Trust committed itself to the idea that it wasn't enough to simply state that it is possible for schools to do better by children of color and children from low-income families; it needed to demonstrate that there are schools that actually *do* better.

Ed Trust hired me in 2004 to help find such schools, and it has afforded me an amazing opportunity ever since to learn from educators who have faced down some of the biggest issues we have in education today. I am enormously grateful to Ed Trust and its founder Kati Haycock for this opportunity.

That said, neither Ed Trust nor Kati should be held responsible for what I have written in this book. It is my work, and whatever errors of judgment or fact it contains belong solely to me.

I said I have had the chance to learn from an amazing set of educators, and I want to thank them from the bottom of my heart. Some—such as Barbara Adderley, Jennie Black, Debbie Bolden, Gary Brittingham, Sharon Brittingham, John Capozzi, June Eressy, Deb Gustafson, Ricci Hall, Melissa Mitchell, and Terri Tomlinson—have helped educate me over many years, and they all make an appearance in this book. Others, such as Kennard Branch, Susan Bunting, Sergio Garcia, Craig Gfeller, Jennifer Robbins, and Vincent Romano, are more recent acquaintances but no less important for that.

Still others are not named in this book but nonetheless have helped shape my thinking. I want to thank Meridith Bang and Beth John and the other folks from Pass Christian, Mississippi; Mary Haynes-Smith and her amazing team at Bethune Elementary in New Orleans; Conrad Lopes, Denise Garison, and the folks at Jack Britt High School in Fayetteville, North Carolina; Cecilia Sanchez and her team at Dr. Carlos J. Finlay Elementary in Miami; the folks at Menlo Park Elementary in Portland, Oregon; the team at Ware Elementary; Bonnie Hess and the folks at Chadwick Elementary in Baltimore County, Maryland; TerriAnn Phillips and her team at DeQueen Elementary; Arelis Diaz, Mary Lang, Michelle Krynicki, Bill Fetterhoff, and the other folks in North Godwin, Michigan; Dan St. Louis and the others at University Park Campus School; Lisa Tabarez and her team at Imperial High School in Imperial, California; Melinda Young and the folks in Steubenville, Ohio; Cynthia Kulhman and the wonderful folks at Charles Drew Charter School in Atlanta; John Daniels and Teri Brecheen of Cottonwood, Oklahoma, and the intrepid reading teachers of Oklahoma; Jeffrey Litt and the folks at Carl Icahn Charter School in the Bronx, New York; Kimberley Steadman and the thoughtful folks at Brooke Charter School in Boston; Pete Routhier and the folks at Brimley Elementary School in Michigan; Sheri Shirley and the dogged folks at Oakland Heights Elementary in Arkansas; Tom Graham and the folks at Griegos Elementary in Albuquerque; Valarie Lewis, Elain Thompson, Von Shepard, Jane Kahan, Keith Jones, Frank Lozier, Susan Brooks, Carmen Macchia, Lucille Keaton, Salvador Rosales, Dolores Cisneros Emerson, George Albano, Francine Castillo, Marty Creel. . . . I'm terrified I have forgotten someone, but in the course of writing this book, I thought of all of them and tried to channel the wisdom they have shared with me over the years.

Three people in particular have been part of my thinking from the very beginning of this book and helped me wrestle through some of the questions that I wanted to address: Ricardo LeBlanc-Esparza, Diane Scricca, and Molly Bensinger-Lacy, who helped me more than I had any right to expect or ask. Molly kept me on track and provided a lighthouse when I floundered in a foggy sea of thought.

Deep thanks also to Harvard Education Press's Doug Clayton and Nancy Walser for pushing me to write this book and providing encouragement and helpful nudges in the right direction, and the production team who brought the whole thing into reality.

And, finally, my love and thanks to my family and friends who—I am sorry to say—put up with a lot of neglect while I was writing this book.

—Karin Chenoweth
Silver Spring, Maryland, 2016

About the Author

KARIN CHENOWETH is author of *It's Being Done: Academic Success in Unexpected Schools* (2007), *HOW It's Being Done: Urgent Lessons from Unexpected Schools* (2009), and co-author of *Getting It Done: Leading Academic Success in Unexpected Schools* (2011), all published by Harvard Education Press. A longtime education writer, she has written for a wide range of publications, including the *Huffington Post,* the *Washington Post, Education Week, Black Issues In Higher Education* (now *Diverse*), *Kappan,* and *Educational Leadership.* Since 2004, she has been writer-in-residence at The Education Trust.

Index

performance of, 32–33, 36
racism experienced by, 72–73, 81
schools serving, 3, 6, 7
Mitchell, Melissa, 89, 90–91
monitoring systems, 193–196
morning assemblies, 152
multigrade classes, 163

NAEP. *See* National Assessment of
Educational Progress
Napier, Will, 31
Nassau County, 37
National Assessment of Educational
Progress (NAEP), 12–13, 14
Nickerson, Dominique, 41–42
No Child Left Behind (NCLB), 13, 15,
106, 172
Nolan, Patrick, 46, 48

O'Donnell, Kate, 132
on-campus suspension room (OCS), 24
outliers, 2, 3
over scheduling, 39
Owens, Jay, 177

Palutzke, Stephani, 30
PARCC assessment, 14–15, 129
parents
information systems for, 145–147
low-income, 92
relationship building with, 91–92
school relations and, 22
Parker, Dennis, 27–29
Parker, Marie, 132, 133
Perez, Cecilia, 30
performance measures, 2
See also assessments
physical environment, 87, 88, 93, 118,
138, 192

planning time, 64–65, 94, 107–108,
128, 134
postsecondary education, 29–30, 38,
114, 149
Prince William County, 133
principals
See also specific principals
appointment of, 170
district administration and, 76–77,
169–178
importance of, 4–5, 133
involvement of, 46–47, 71–72, 75
training of, 195–196
professional development, 5, 23, 63,
65–66, 69–70, 95, 108, 116–118,
135, 154, 172, 191–192, 202
professional learning communities,
134, 148, 172, 177
proficiency rates, 15

racism, 72–73, 81
reading achievement, 12–13, 14
Reading Counts, 160–161
reading instruction, 148–149,
153–154, 160–161, 186
recognition, systems of, 190–192
relationship building, 196–198
remedial classes, 63, 184
resiliency, 33
restorative justice, 24–25
Ricca, Rose Linda, 48, 49–50
Robbins, Jennifer, 161–162,
165–166
Romano, Vincent, 39, 41–47,
49–54, 57, 77–80, 191
Roulston, William, 148

safety issues, 148
Saturday detentions, 43